A Taste of Le Sud

A collection of recipes and wine pairings from

La Maison du Rire

Wine and Food School in the Corbières

Emma Kershaw

Photography by Garth Bowden

Front cover photography with kind permission
from Domaine des Soulanes

ISBN number: 978-2-9564583-0-2

Graphic design: **KAT** kevinatrent.com

Contents

La Maison du Rire 1
The wine region, the Languedoc-Roussillon 2
Matching wine with food 8
Tapenade - Olive and anchovy dip 14
Carpaccio de courgettes - Courgette carpaccio 16
Velouté froid de courgettes au chèvre frais - Chilled courgette and goat's cheese velouté 19
Pesto aux fanes de radis - Radish leaf pesto 20
Rillettes de truite - Coarse trout paté 23
Brandade de Nîmes - Salt cod from Nîmes 24
Accras de morue - Salt cod balls 26
Gazpacho - Chilled tomato soup 28
Caviar d'aubergine - Aubergine purée 33
Baba ghanoush 35
Empanadillas au thon - Spicy tuna pastries 36
Tielle Sétoise - Octopus and tomato pies from Sète 38
Salade de lentilles vertes - Green lentil salad 40
Patatas Espagnoles - Spanish potatoes 43
Zarzuela - Catalan fish stew 45
Encornets farcis - Stuffed cuttlefish 47
Thon à la plancha - Chargrilled tuna 49
Brochette de lotte au romarin - Rosemary monkfish skewers 51
Chorizo aux pois chiches - Chickpeas and chorizo 52
Chorizo flambé - Flambéed chorizo and peppers 55
Soubressade - Spicy sausage tapas 56
Brochette et coustellous de porc à la plancha - Pork two ways 58
Boles de Picolat - Catalan meatballs 61
Magret de canard sauce Carignan - Duck breast with a Carignan sauce 64
Gigot d'agneau à la cuillère - Slow roast lamb with lentils 66
Gâteau aux amandes - Almond cake 69
Soupe de fraises - Strawberry soup 70
Pain d'épice - Spiced cake 72
Petits pots au chocolat - Chocolate pots 73
Petits carrés au chocolat - Chocolate fruit and nut squares 75
Pruneaux enrobés de chocolat - Chocolate prunes 76
List of wine producers 78
Photography 80

La Maison du Rire
Wine and Food School in the Corbières
www.lamaisondurire.com
0033 (0)4 68 33 07 61

La Maison du Rire

I created La Maison du Rire to share my passion for the wines and the foods of the Languedoc-Roussillon. For more years than I care to admit I have been teaching about the world of wine, from beginner level to Wine & Spirit Education Trust (WSET) Diploma. Over the years I have worked with many chefs and restaurateurs partnering wine and food. I have always maintained that regardless of whether you are a professional or an amateur, wines are much better tasted, and appreciated, when partnered with food. The perfect match can make a meal, and indeed a memory.

In 2010 I moved permanently to the Corbières, where, together with my husband Chris, we renovated an old, dilapidated winery to create 'La Maison du Rire', a school about the wines and the gastronomy of the Languedoc-Roussillon. Here I teach a wide range of courses about the wines and foods of this incredibly diverse region. It is also our family home which we share with our little boy Louis, a tractor driver in the making.

The Languedoc-Roussillon, a region much maligned in the past, has in fact a rich history in gastronomy, and is of course one of the largest wine regions in the world. It is, in my opinion, one of the most diverse wine regions there is. With an incredible range of grape varieties, from indigenous to classic, a diversity of climate, soil, topography and of the people creating the wines.

I fell in love with this wonderful region many, many years ago and it is my delight to be able to share my discoveries with wine lovers from across the globe. It is indeed thanks to these students that this book was created. Such kind comments regarding the food that I made and served at tastings, and so many of you asking me to create a recipe book. So to those of you that asked me for my recipes; here they are at long last.

The recipes are a combination of originals and my own take on some classic dishes. My belief is that recipes should be a guideline rather than a definitive instruction. So here you will find that I encourage you to experiment and use your palate as a guide.* Cooking is an organic process and there are times when you need to trust yourself to add extra salt/spice/wine to the dish.

All recipes are for a tapas sized portion for eight, or a starter sized portion for four, unless otherwise stated.

Always use the best possible ingredients that you can. I am a great believer in following seasons and buying local, fresh food responsibly where possible. It does make a difference to the taste of the dish if you have used fruits and vegetables that are ripe and in season rather than the dull, plastic wrapped, imported versions often found in the supermarket. Embrace what is local to you and adapt recipes accordingly. The eggs I use are always free range and large, the butter salted, the fish sustainable and the meat from small, rather than industrial sized, farms. It is sometimes impossible to avoid 'la grande surface' (the supermarkets) and organic does not always make sense, but if we all try to support our local shops and farms I believe that the world will be a better place.

The purpose of these recipes is to highlight the fabulous ingredients and the wines that I have discovered, and enjoyed from this region. Each recipe has a wine match chosen from the vast range of wines found in the Languedoc-Roussillon. Some are exported internationally and others you will need to make the journey here to experience. With over 21,373 wine estates I have barely scratched the surface of what is available. Just enough to give a taste.

Good food and wine should be celebrated, enjoyed together amongst friends and family.

Life is too short to drink bad wine and not be laughing!

Bon appétit et santé!

Emma x

* It is worth noting that if you change a recipe too much you will throw the wine match out and have to find your own

The wine region, the Languedoc-Roussillon

To try to describe in any detail the wine region of the Languedoc-Roussillon in these few short pages is an impossible task and one that I will not attempt. There are many fine books that you can reference. Instead I will try to give an overall view and understanding of this fabulous region, the wines produced here and the wonderful people that make them.

Geography

The region stretches across 27,000 square kilometres of land, covering the four departments of the Aude, the Hérault, the Gard and the Pyrénées-Orientale in the newly (since 2016) named Occitanie department in the South of France. It starts in the north of the region just west of Nîmes, then continues south to the seaside town of Banyuls sur Mer near the Spanish border, and stretches inland past the romantic city of Carcassonne towards Castlenaudray.

Facts and figures

The Languedoc-Roussillon is one of the largest wine producing regions in the world. There are 245,965 hectares of land planted with grape vines. The region boasts seven 'Cru' appellations, plus 27 Appellation d'Origine Protégée (AOP) in the Languedoc and a further 14 in the Roussillon, then 25 Indication Géographique Protégée (IGP) wines.

In 2009 the classification system for wines in France was updated; AOP replaced Appellation d'Origine Contrôlée (AOC), IGP replaced Vins de Pays (VdP) and Vin de France replaced the Table Wine category. Today rather confusingly, you may see bottles labelled with either classification until the old system is finally phased out.

The situation is changing and being updated all the time, and by the time this book goes to print there will undoubtedly be new appellations added to the list. This region produces a staggering 1.8 billion bottles of wine annually, which equates to 5% of the world's total wine production. One in every three bottles of French wine produced comes from the Languedoc-Roussillon*.

How it all began

This is France's oldest wine region. The vines were first planted in and around Narbonne on the Mediterranean coast in 5th century BC by the Greeks and the Etruscans, having discovered in the Languedoc the perfect climate and terrain for vines. Later when the Romans expanded their growing empire they introduced more vines across the region and before long the Languedoc, and its wines from Narbonne, was one of the key suppliers to Rome and its Empire.

Then in AD 92 things changed. Disliking the popularity and dominance of these wines in his Empire the Emperor Domitian issued an edict forbidding any new plantings and scrubbed up many of the vines planted in and around Narbonne. The area lost over half of its vineyard plantings at this time. However the Church in France realised the importance of the vine as a source of wealth and influence. So it stepped in and saved these vines, buying the land and taking over wine production. Soon a network of abbeys and monasteries became the epicentre of viticulture and vinification within the Languedoc and the region fast became known for producing high quality wines especially from the vineyards around Saint Chinian and St Guilhem-le-Désert. **

In the early middle ages France was not the unified country it now is. The Languedoc, like many other regions, was broken into a series of independent states. It had its own language which exists to this day, Occitan. The langue d'Oc as it was called, translates as the language of 'yes' and gives the region its name; 'Languedoc'. This was the period of the Cathars, a secular group that eventually were wiped out by the Catholics. Further south at this time, the Roussillon was part of the Spanish kingdom of Catalunya-Aragon. The Roussillon was, as it still is, heavily influenced by the Catalan culture. Today the language, Catalan, is still spoken and seen all over. The food comprises tapas dishes heavily flavoured with tomatoes, peppers, paprika, piment d'espelette and chorizo sausages. Then the wines are made with Spanish varietals such as Cencibel (Tempranillo), Grenache and Macabeu. All still very Catalan in style despite the Roussillon having left Catalunya to become French in 1659.

A poor reputation

Yet modern history has not been kind to the Languedoc-Roussillon and it has long been tainted with a poor image, as that of a region of 'quantity over quality'. For many years it was considered too hot and dry to produce any wines of excellence; churning out syrupy, baked and alcoholic styles.

This reputation for producing vast quantities of bulk wines has been hard to shake. Historically it was fitting, as during the 19th century a French factory worker would be paid a daily quota of six litres a day for males, and 4 litres a day for women! They would have been basic wines produced in the Languedoc-Roussillon and sold 'en vrac' (in bulk). By the turn of the century, when these somewhat excessive payments in the factories were stopped there was now so much cheap wine available with much less demand. The bars and restaurants across France had to sell the wines at a massively reduced price to try and shift it. The majority of these wines came from the Languedoc-Roussillon, the so-called bulk wine region of France.

* All figures from Conseil Interprofessionnel des vins AOC du Languedoc et des IGP Sud de France

** Historical references taken from www.languedoc-aoc.com

The 20th century was the heyday for mass production in the Languedoc-Roussillon. The land had already been heavily planted with fast growing varieties to produce easy drinking wines. Grape varieties such as Carignan, Cinsault, Aramon and Alicante Bouchet were planted alongside the better quality Grenache and Mourvèdre. Monoculture was the order of the day with field upon field of vines planted. The caves cooperatives dominated, producing 95% of the wines made. Consumption was high, very high. Wine featured heavily in the daily life of the average French family during the 1960s when the average consumption per capita peaked at over 150 litres in a year. Compare that to two bottles a year in the UK during that same period!

Over production

However the tide was changing and the excessive production and heavy discounting of these rough and ready wines led to the new generation in the 1970s shunning wine and turning to more trendy drinks such as beers and cocktails instead. So consumption and demand slumped.

What followed was years of wine production that was surplus to requirement, creating the 'wine lake'. In the 1980s a wave of new wine making countries entered the international wine market. Australia, California and South Africa came with their quality, fruit driven wines and their friendly winemakers. International markets were beginning to turn their backs on the outdated wine regions such as the Languedoc-Roussillon with their varying quality of wines, preferring instead the new exciting wines from the New World.

Reducing the quantity

Then in the decade from 2000 the EU endeavoured to reduce this mass over-production in regions such as the LanguedocRoussillon. They did what was called a sponsored vine-pull. Paying for the poor quality vines that produced these dull wines to be pulled up and replanted with fruit and olive trees. So moving away from the monoculture of the 20th century back to the original polyculture; a diverse planting of vines, olives, fruit trees and forests.

This resulted in an important shrinkage of the vineyard area planted. A massive 27% was scrubbed up by the end of this exercise. This had the benefit of not only reducing the over production, but also of improving the overall quality of wines produced here. Quality that had always existed but was hard to find amongst the mass of simple wines. Many of the caves cooperatives now found it hard to survive and were forced to close their doors. A new generation of wine makers appeared. They had studied the science of oenology in universities and travelled to other wine regions across the globe. They were informed and they were passionate. Taking over the family estates many moved away from the caves cooperatives, shunning the wine styles of their fathers and grandfathers. They wanted to prove themselves in the world of wine, they wanted to see all of their hard work in the vineyards pay off in the bottle. They knew, as did the ancient Greeks, that the Languedoc-Roussillon had all the raw ingredients needed to make outstanding wines.

A new beginning

Slowly but surely the region has been shedding that 'poor quality, vast quantity' reputation. The region has some of the lowest yields in France, often as little as 25 hectolitres per hectare (hl/ha), compared to 48hl/ha for some of the most expensive wines in the world that hail from Bordeaux. Consider that low yields are often linked to quality; low yields in wine grapes equate to intensity of flavour as opposed to high yields which create dilute flavours. Less is more in the world of wine, the fewer the grapes the better the quality of wine is a general rule of thumb. Surely then the Languedoc-Roussillon must be considered capable of producing high quality wines.

Today the Languedoc-Roussillon is one of the most exciting and vibrant wine regions in the world. It is incredibly diverse, with an impressive range of topography, geology, climates and microclimates, of grape varieties and of people! All creating an unrivalled selection of wine styles.

Influences and styles

What makes this region so diverse? It is the influence of the mountain ranges determining the climate and what might grow there; the Pyrenees, the Montagne Noir and the Cévennes. It is the complexity of soils; ranging from vast pebble terraces, sandstone to calcareous clay, limestone and shale, clayey soils, pudding stone, sandy soils and schist to name but a few. Each contributes a different characteristic to the final product. It is the Mediterranean climate – hot, sunny, windy and generally dry – which is ideal for grape growing, and the lack of mildew which aids organic and biodynamic viticulture. It is the long lineage of grape varieties grown here ranging from the classics (such as Cabernet Sauvignon) to the almost unknown (Lledonner Pelut). It is the passionate and devoted people crafting these wines. Those born into winemaking families where the estates have been passed down from generation to generation, and then generation again. It is the new comers arriving from foreign shores or other regions of France, eager to make their mark. It is the many wines produced from tiny wine domaines; fine wines that are so individual in character. Produced from gnarly, old vines, and made in minuscule quantities. It is the internationally appealing wines that are made in modern, slick wineries, all shiny and gleaming with the latest technology.

In a nutshell

So with all this diversity how do I explain the wines of the Languedoc-Roussillon in a succinct manner? I could tell you that it is a region that produces predominately red wines. That is true, but I have found over the years that some of the most exciting wines that I have tasted here are actually white wines produced from a selection of strangely named grape varieties indigenous to this part of the world. I could also generalise and say that they are all big flavoured, bold and alcoholic wines, especially those from the scorched vineyards of the Roussillon. And yet there is a movement away from that style. A new wave of exciting winemakers making deliciously elegant wines, that are both complex and full of flavour yet restrained, without the heavy whack of alcohol and jammy fruit traditionally found here.

Photograph with kind permission from Domaine des Soulanes

I would say that this a region in the throes of change. Trying to shed its poor reputation of yesteryear with a potential for producing outstanding wines capable of equalling, bettering even, some of the great wines of the world.

So next time you head to the wine shop aim for the section labelled the South of France and pick up a bottle of one of the many fine wines available from the Languedoc-Roussillon and enjoy a taste of le sud!

The grape varieties

This list is far from exhaustive as there are so many different varieties grown in the Languedoc-Roussillon but I have named the key players. The majority of the appellation wines are made from a blend of two or more varieties, with some exceptions.

Red and rosé varieties

Carignan – a grape variety that is capable of producing great wines as more and more producers are proving. However it is important to keep yields low and site selection is key to producing wines of quality that are capable of prolonged ageing. The characteristics are dark fruits, pronounced tannins and a gamey, spicy flavour.

Cinsault – predominately used for rosé wines here. It has a thin skin and can be prone to disease. However it brings a lovely fresh acidity and a perfumed red fruit character to the wines.

Grenache Noir – originally from Spain, produces wines with red fruit character, violet aromas and high alcohol. Used as part of the blend in dry, red wines and for the sweet, fortified wines from Banyuls, Maury and Rivesaltes.

Mourvèdre – a quality grape often used as an 'improver' in blends. With high tannins and a blackcurrant fruit character; it is a grape that ages well becoming more complex and interesting with maturation. Planted along the Mediterranean coast, Mourvèdre is a grape that likes its feet in the sand and its head in the sun!

Syrah – another of the so-called 'improver' varieties. Introduced to the Languedoc-Roussillon from the neighbouring Rhône Valley and since the 1980s its popularity has spread rapidly. It has pronounced tannin and acidity, dark fruits and a peppery spice. It marries well with oak and can produce wines of great longevity.

Other varieties – Cabernet Sauvignon, Cabernet Franc, Fer Servadou, Lledonner Pelut (Hairy Grenache), Malbec (Cot), Marselan, Merlot, Pinot Noir, Piquepoul Noir and Terret Noir.

White varieties

Bourboulenc – a late ripening variety that has high acidity with key aromas of citrus fruits and smoke. Particularly found in the white wines of La Clape.

Grenache Blanc – part of the large Grenache family, it is prone to over yielding and then it produces flabby, rather dull wines. However if the yields are kept under control it can contribute a citrus and herbaceous character to the blend, with a good longevity.

Grenache Gris – a rising star especially in the southerly vineyards of the Roussillon. A pink skinned variety, it produces high quality whites wines with delicious aromas of peaches and apricot fruits, acacia blossom with a long mineral finish. Used as a single varietal as well as part of a blend.

Marsanne – usually seen partnered with Roussanne. It produces a deeply coloured, nutty and spicy wine with hints of pear that can be oak aged. A variety that benefits ageing where it will become more complex, honeyed and intensely flavoured.

Roussanne – as the name implies it is famous for the russet colour of the grapes when ripe. A floral, slightly herbaceous nose that gives a wine full in flavour, with hints of pear, honey and spice.

Vermentino – also known as Rolle, grown all along the Mediterranean coast and in increasing amounts here in the Languedoc-Roussillon. Producing wines with crunchy, citrus fruits, a steely mineral character and a sometimes slightly saline finish.

Macabeu – also known as Macabeo or Viura. Catalan in origin this variety is increasing in popularity in the vineyards of the Roussillon. Used for both dry and dessert wines, it has a high alcohol and a grapefruit aroma, however it can often be lacking in acidity so is best in blends.

Muscat à Petits Grains – this is the quality grape used for the Vins Doux Naturel, sweet fortified wines that are a speciality here. Pale, yellow skinned with a fabulous floral, grapey aroma and flavour.

Other varieties – Chardonnay, Chenin Blanc, Clairette Blanche, Mauzac, Piquepoul Blanc, Sauvignon Blanc, Terret Blanc, Ugni Blanc and Viognier.

The Appellations

The Languedoc Crus

Corbières-Boutenac AOC
Faugères AOC
La Clape AOC
Minervois-La Livinière AOC
Pic Saint Loup AOC
Saint-Chinian Berlou AOC
Saint-Chinian Roquebrun AOC

The AOC/AOPs

Languedoc

Cabardès AOC
Clairette du Languedoc AOC
Corbières AOC, Fitou AOC
Languedoc AOC – Cabrières
Languedoc AOC – Grés de Montpellier
Languedoc AOC – La Méjanelle
Languedoc AOC – Montpeyroux
Languedoc AOC – Pézenas
Languedoc AOC – Quatourze
Languedoc AOC – Saint-Christol
Languedoc AOC – Saint-Drézéry
Languedoc AOC – Saint-Georges-d'Orques
Languedoc AOC – Saint-Saturnin
Languedoc AOC – Sommières
Limoux AOC
Malepère AOC
Muscat de Frontignan AOC
Muscat de Lunel AOC
Muscat de Mireval AOC
Muscat de Saint-Jean-de-Minervois AOC
Minervois AOC
Picpoul de Pinet AOP
Saint-Chinian AOC
Terrasses du Larzac AOC
Blanquette de Limoux AOC
Crémant de Limoux AOC

Roussillon

Collioure AOC
Côtes du Roussillon AOC
Côtes du Roussillon Villages AOC
Côtes du Roussillon Villages Caramany AOC
Côtes du Roussillon Villages Latour de France AOC
Côtes du Roussillon Villages Lesquerde AOC
Côtes du Roussillon Villages Tautavel AOC
Côtes du Roussillon Villages Les Aspres AOC
Maury sec AOC
Rivesaltes VDN AOC
Maury VDN AOC
Banyuls VDN AOC
Banyuls Grand Cru VDN AOC
Muscat de Rivesaltes VDN AOC

The above AOC's as listed by the Conseil Interprofessionnel des Vins du Languedoc and the Conseil Interprofessionnel des Vins du Roussillon (CIVR)

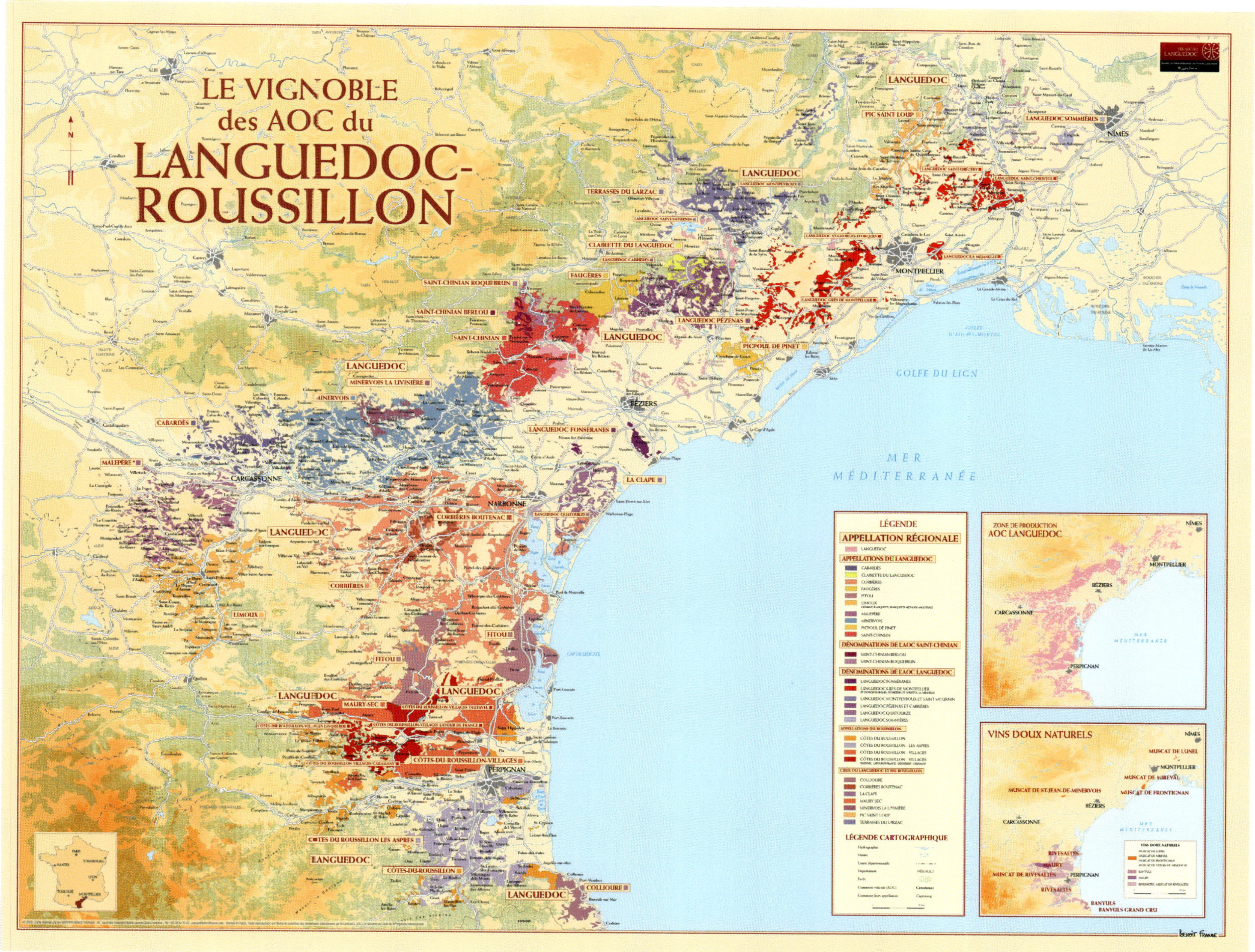

Map with kind permission from Éditions Benoit France

Matching wine with food

There are many books that have been written about the complexities of wine and food matching and it is a subject that is as fascinating as it is confusing. Whilst personal preference plays a strong part in what we choose and what we enjoy, it is not always the best indicator for finding a perfect match. Most of us will have a preference for a certain style of food and possibly for a specific colour of wine. However they do not always work well together and you might find yourself eating the food and drinking the wines as almost two separate entities. A good match can make a meal. It can create a powerful memory, not to be forgotten. A bad match can sour the experience, quite literally. It can also influence your opinion about a wine and your enjoyment of the food.

I had my first perfect wine and food moment in Le Touquet many years ago, in a restaurant overlooking the sea. I was with my parents and we were having dessert. I am not usually a great pudding eater having more of a savoury palate, but on this occasion I had chosen a tartlet of summer red berries and the waiter recommended a glass of Bugey* wine to go with it. I had no idea what it was at the time but happily accepted his recommendation. I think my father was a little bemused as my parents did not drink sweet wines; it must have seemed very hedonistic!

When it came it was a vibrant pink, frothy, fizzy wine. Deliciously sweet and full of the same summer berry flavours that were on my plate. It was a match made in heaven. I am not so sure that I convinced my father of that just then but he enjoyed seeing my pleasure! It was for me a light bulb moment and the beginning of a much loved career in seeking out those perfect matches and teaching about the fascinating subject of wine and food pairing.

Whilst I have always enjoyed the challenge of working with wine and food and teaching my findings, I am aware that it is a subject that can sometimes lead to pomposity and getting bogged down in the minutiae of detail when all you want to do is have a plate of good food and a decent glass of wine. So I have done my best to avoid that and have put together some guidelines to help direct you in the art and science of harmonising food with wine. I hope you enjoy your culinary and vinous voyage as much as I have (and do) mine!

Some guidelines

A simplistic method is to match like for like. This involves pairing compatible elements in both the food and the wine. Similar flavours, for example an aged Pinot Noir with mushroomy, gamey notes works very well with wild mushrooms. Unfortunately whilst this is a fairly easy rule to adopt it doesn't always follow through and there are of course exceptions! For example, spicy and spicy can on occasion be too much. It can create a big explosion of flavours in your mouth that fight with each other rather than creating a harmonising experience.

Sometimes, you might look for a complementary match that is contrasting rather than congruent. An instance where the flavours and tastes are balanced by their differences. To illustrate this point, imagine a cheese fondue which has a creamy fatty character and then partner it with an acidic Rousette de Savoie. Here the acidity is contrasting yet complementary to the richness of the cheese, cutting through the fattiness and refreshing the palate.

There are also times when opposites attract. A salty blue cheese partnered with a sweet wine is a classic example. The sweetness in the wine has a cancellation effect on the food, in that it reduces the perception of extreme saltiness and creates a much more enjoyable experience. Which is why we often pair sweet and savoury foods together; ham with a honey glaze, Cheddar and chutney, roast duck with a cherry sauce.

Here I have highlighted some of the key elements that you might want to consider and explain their effect on both the wine and the food.

Acidity

The acidity in the wine needs to match, or be a superior to, that of the dish otherwise the wine will taste flat and dull. This is why wines that might appear too acidic as a stand-alone drink come into their element when partnered correctly. A pork dish served with a tart, redcurrant sauce will need a wine with high acidity to match that of the sauce, whereas pork and sage will need a less acidic wine. Acidity in the food can come from lemons, vinegar, fruit, or possibly a wine reduction in the sauce, and their acidic strength will vary. It is worth noting that vinegar should be used with restraint if you are planning to serve a quality wine as it is generally not very wine friendly. It causes many wines to turn vinegary in taste, which is not really a taste we want in a wine!

Tannin

Whilst food does not need tannin it is true that certain foods work very well with tannic wines, because these wines will have other characteristics that complement the dish. Some foods can soften the tannins, which in turn rounds out the wine and enhances the fruit flavours. Due to its protein content, red meat in

Bugey Cerdon is semi sweet, sparkling rosé wine from the Jura region in eastern France. Made from Gamay and Poulsard grapes, it produces a 'grapey' flavoured wine with a deep pink colour. It is made in the méthode ancestrale, this same method that produced the first ever sparkling wines in a Benedictine monastery just outside of the Languedocian town of Limoux in 1531.

particular can tone down the tannins in a wine. Hence the old adage of red wine with red meat. Conversely certain foods can extract the tannins making them more obvious and even render the wine bitter. Oily fish with a full-bodied, tannic red is a perfect example of a match made in hell.

Key components

Determine the strongest element of the dish. This is important when harmonising wine and food, and it may not always be obvious. Sometimes it will be the protein that needs to be matched; the meat, fish or lentils. Other times it could be the sauce which may be sweet, creamy, herby or spicy. Or it could be the cooking method. There is a significant difference in the taste and weight of a dish depending on how it has been cooked. Take chicken as an example; poached, grilled, fried, roasted or barbecued the humble bird will require quite different wines depending on how it has been handled.

Matching the origin

Wines and dishes that come from the same area often work very well together as they have been created in the same environment with each other in mind. For example; moules marinières and Muscadet, foie gras and Sauternes, a Bolognese sauce with a Lambrusco, Picpoul de Pinet and fresh oysters.

Wine or food

Which is the most important? There will be occasions when you have been saving a special bottle. So in that case the wine takes priority and you will need to take into account its age and style, and choose your menu accordingly. Sometimes it might be the dish; a favourite recipe or the new season's asparagus, and in that case the wine will be chosen to partner the food.

So often we forget this and excitedly open a bottle that we have been saving without great due care and attention to the food served. Then, instead of the meal being memorable for the pleasure it bought, it is a disappointment. That very special bottle actually tasted rather ordinary.

Spice

This is a huge subject in itself but to summarise it is worth noting that spices are divided into three categories:

Sweet-spicy – cinnamon, clove, nutmeg, ginger and tamarind

Savoury-spicy – cumin, pepper, cardamom and fish sauce

Hot-spicy – chilli, mustard seed, hot peppers and horseradish

However, often there will be a cross-over of these spices so a general rule of thumb is that wines low in alcohol, with crisp acidity, soft tannins and little to no oak work best. Choose wines with a good fruit content to balance the spice, and in some cases a touch of residual sugar helps soften the heat of the chilli whilst not over powering the food, a case of a complementary pairing. Still, go easy, a dessert wine is not recommended, that would be a step too far and too much of a contrast.

Age

Of the wine not the drinker! Remember that as a wine ages its characteristics and flavours change. A red wine becomes more delicate, the primary fruits are replaced with secondary aromas such as dried fruits, cigar, cedar, with gamey and fungal tones. Whilst a white wine will become less aromatic and take on nutty, buttery, and in some cases, honeyed tones. So that the food match that worked so well in the wine's youthful state will not necessarily work so well once the wine is aged.

Generally the rule of thumb is that the older the wine the simpler the dish because an aged wine is delicate and cannot withstand the bold flavours of spice and fusion cooking. For instance a simple roast lamb served with an aged Pauillac, is an elegant symphony.

Experiment!

Today's cooking, as with today's wine making, is very varied. Blind tasting where the taster can pinpoint a wine to the exact vineyard, is much harder now in a world of 'international' winemaking styles. A shame perhaps. Cooking also borrows from one cuisine to another; French with hints of Japanese, Italian combined with Thai ingredients.

What we lose in identity we gain in new experiences. It opens the door to experimentation. Wine and food pairing combinations that of old would not have worked and so would not have been considered, can now be enjoyed. For example red wines with fish – just remember the point about tannin. In fact some fishes, such as tuna, work far better with a light-bodied, chilled red than they do with a white wine. An oak aged white wine made from a Marsanne/Roussane blend served with a steak in a creamy mushroom sauce can work surprisingly well.

Sweetness

One of the hard and fast rules in wine and food pairing is that the wine's sweetness must match, or exceed, that of the dessert. A sweet dish with a dry wine will rip all the fruit character from the wine and render it acidic (or tannic if red) with very little else left to recommend it.

Choosing which dessert wine to partner with the dessert course can be one of the most complicated matches to get right. It is also the one that is often ignored as it is at the end of the meal. Interestingly, I find that more than with any other style of wine, sweet wines divide opinion greatly in the tastings that I hold. They lost their fashionable status twenty years or so ago and it has been a slow return. Many people just do not appreciate the style and avoid them altogether. However it is worth venturing into the world of 'sticky wines' as there are some absolutely fantastic examples being made all over the world. The Vins Doux Naturel (VDN) from the Languedoc-Roussillon, the botrytis affected wines of Jurançon, Montbazillac and the Eisweins from Germany to name but a few. The key is the getting the perfect balance of sweetness and acidity in the wine.

So where do we start with getting that all important perfect match when there are so many different desserts and so many variations of sweet wines? Well that is a book in itself, but as a guide fruit-based desserts are the easiest to match as they combine both sweetness and acidity, both of which are found in many of the classic dessert wines such as Sauternes, Coteaux du Layon and Riesling Ausleses.

Chocolate on the other hand coats the palate and can be a real wine killer. If it is a light chocolate mousse then something like a Moscato d'Asti works very well, with its fruity, frothy character and light alcohol. With a rich chocolate fondant I would lean towards the rich, red VDNs from the south of France, a Maury or a Rasteau from the Rhône valley, which combine both sweetness and alcohol.

Then with ice-cream we have to contend with the double whammy of very sweet and very cold. A Blanquette Ancestrale or other sweet sparkling wine just about manages the task.

Egg based desserts require a wine that is mild in flavour, light and buttery. A late harvest Pinot Gris from Alsace, for example, with a crème brulée.

Cheese

One of the great myths is that of cheese and red wine working well together. They are (perhaps surprisingly) usually not a very good match. Although we are all guilty of getting out the platter of cheeses at the end of a meal and popping a bottle of red on the table, myself included! But we really shouldn't as it doesn't work.

Again, it is the tannins that get in the way and either over power the cheese, or the cheese causes the tannins to taste bitter. White wines are, on the whole, a far better match with their acidity and buttery characteristics. However one wine to match all cheeses just does not exist. There are far too many flavours and elements to consider. It is best to be selective and just offer one or two very fine cheeses rather than a Smörgåsbord of 10 or 12.

A mature Comté or Cheddar works best with a buttery Chardonnay or another full-bodied oak aged white. At a push a fruity Cabernet or Zinfandel could work, but be wary of their tannins. Brie and Camembert can be partnered with a young Chardonnay or a youthful Pinot Noir.

Blue cheeses need sweet wines to balance the saltiness: this is a case of opposites attracting and the sweetness in the wine cancelling the salt in the cheese as already explained. Either a red such as Port with Stilton or a white, for instance Sauternes with Roquefort. Goat's cheese works well with aromatic white wines, in particular Sauvignon Blanc based wines.

So called difficult foods

There are some foods that are harder to match than others. Artichokes are notorious for making dry wines appear sweet, and asparagus for turning everything metallic. Eggs and chocolate are coaters. Soup is too liquid. Curry and chillies can overpower and strip the fruit from the wine. Ice-cream is too cold. Vinegar renders everything in the glass to its level! And so on. ut all of these so called difficulties can be overcome and all these foods can be partnered very well with the right wine, as shown in this book.

In a restaurant

Imagine you are in a restaurant having a meal and there are several of you having different dishes, and you have been given the task of selecting the wine. Which wine should you choose? Call the sommelier! Seriously, if there is one, this is the perfect time to hand over. It's their job and they know their wines and menus inside out. Another alternative would be to choose wines by the glass. More and more establishments are offering a varied and exciting range by the glass. It is worth checking how they preserve their wines by the glass though, as a poorly kept wine will be oxidised and unpleasant to drink.

However, neither of those scenarios may be relevant so in that case I would recommend going for a lightly aromatic white and a fruity red. These wines are crowd pleasers and won't have a detrimental effect on the food or the ambiance. It may not be the perfect match but it will be the perfect party!

To conclude, a great wine and food pairing is really just about creating balance and harmony between the food and the wine. So despite all the complexities of the different elements above, wine was made to partner food! Remember to enjoy the experience and not get bogged down in the detail.

Tapenade – Olive and anchovy dip

The classic dish of the south: a pungent combination of olives, anchovies from Collioure, capers, garlic, herbs and olive oil. A little goes along way; it is traditionally served on toasts or with crudités as an apéro but can also be used as a base for tomato tarts. A spoonful can be added to sauces to add a richness. You can make it vegetarian or vegan by replacing the anchovies with sun-dried tomatoes, but then it becomes a 'pâte d'olives' rather than a tapenade.

Ingredients

- 200g quality black olives. I often use ones that have been marinated in Herbs de Provence
- 50g quality green olives
- 2–3 anchovy fillets
- 1 tbsp capers, rinsed
- Herbs de Provence
- 2 large garlic cloves, peeled
- Lots of good quality olive oil
- 2 sun dried tomatoes in oil – optional

Method

1. Firstly de-stone the olives. It is worth taking the time to do this as pitted olives never have the same flavour as whole olives bought fresh from the market.
2. Place all of the ingredients, except the oil, in the food processor and pulse gently adding oil as you go.
3. If you are not too sure how strong the anchovies are it is best to start with one or two and add more as you go along as the anchovies from Collioure, the best on the Mediterranean, are very powerful and can dominate the dish. If you find that the anchovies are too dominant try adding a sun dried tomato or two as this can even the flavours out .
4. Add glugs of olive oil as you go until you reach the right consistency – a coarse paste that can be used as a dip or on toast. If you prefer a smoother style then pulse for longer and add more oil.
5. Taste and check the balance for saltiness, herbs and aromatics. Amend to suit your palate.
6. Serve with fresh bread and crudités.

Wine match

This is a pungent dish, salty with a slightly bitter edge and the best wine is a Blanquette de Limoux. Make sure it is Brut, however, as an Ancestrale, (sweeter style), would not do at all. This Mauzac based wine has crisp acidity that cuts through the saltiness, and the effervescence lifts the palate so that the saltiness in the tapenade is softened whilst the flavour of the wine shines through. Domaine Antech Blanquette Réserve is a consistently good match for my tapenade. It is very dry at 1.3g/l residual sugar and the rustic green apple character from the Mauzac shines in a way that Champagne or Prosecco never could!

Green olive tapenade

This is a light, fresher tapenade than the classic version, popular with those that are not so keen on the bitterness of black olives.

Ingredients

- 250g quality green olives
- 2–3 anchovy fillets in olive oil, or 2 salted anchovy fillets thoroughly rinsed
- 1 tbsp capers, rinsed
- 100g whole almonds, skins on
- 1 handful of fresh basil
- 2 large garlic cloves
- Lots of good quality olive oil

Method

1. Follow the same method as above.
2. Serve with fresh bread and crudités.

Wine match

The almonds add a toasty element to this tapenade and so a Chardonnay-dominant Crémant works well here. I have recently discovered and thoroughly enjoyed the Cuvée Oubliée from Maison Antech. This blend of Chardonnay, Chenin and Mauzac has extended lees ageing, hence the oubliée (forgotten) element, which adds to the toasty complexity. Serve at 11°C to open up the aromas. Antech is one of the largest sparkling wine producers of Limoux and has been in the same family for six generations. They specialise in the sparkling Blanquette and Crémant wines and have an extensive range.

Carpaccio de courgettes – Courgette carpaccio

This is always a favourite at tastings, and amongst friends, as it really showcases how fantastic the courgettes are here. They are sweet and fragrant, and it is a dish that looks very pretty. It is also very easy to make, just be careful of your fingers!

Ingredients

- 4 courgettes, a mix of green and yellow, and the younger and smaller the better as they tend to be the sweetest and least bitter
- 1 medium garlic clove very finely minced
- A large handful of fresh basil, roughly chopped
- A small handful of fresh mint, roughly chopped
- Juice of half a small lemon
- 2–4 tbsp quality olive oil, the best you can get. I use a local oil made from the Picholine olives; it is fruity and punchy
- 150g fresh goat's cheese, I buy all my goat's cheese from Jean-Baptiste Carrus, one of the best producers in the region; it is so sublimely soft and creamy
- Salt and pepper to taste

Method

1. This is best started the night before to allow the flavours to marry, but if you are running short of time than allow at least three hours and don't refrigerate.
2. Rinse the courgettes and top and tail, then very carefully slice on the finest setting with a mandolin. Concentration is key here, we are not looking to add any red to the dish!
3. Put the sliced courgettes into a container with a lid, then add the garlic, herbs (saving some for decoration), lemon juice, 2–3 tablespoons of the oil and the seasoning.
4. Pop on the lid and give it a good shake to combine thoroughly, you might find that you need to separate the courgettes with your hands.
5. Leave in the fridge overnight.
6. The following day, a good hour before you intend to eat, take the courgettes out of the fridge and bring up to room temperature.
7. Check the seasoning and spread onto a platter. Remove any brown looking basil or mint at this stage.
8. Crumble on the goat's cheese evenly and drizzle with more olive oil and chopped herbs.
9. Enjoy with plenty of fresh bread to soak up the juices.

Variations

If you are making this in spring time then add a sprinkling of blanched, chopped asparagus and freshly podded peas. The asparagus here tends to be very thick so slice it finely to complement the courgettes.

Wine match

The key elements here are the aromatics of the courgettes and herbs, the creaminess of the goat's cheese and the fruity olive oil. A very successful match was the Domaine Jones' Perle Carignan Gris, an almost unheard of grape variety, only 5ha in France and made in minuscule quantities. It is aromatic and mineral, with the body and depth of flavour needed here. Domaine Jones is found in the southern end of the Languedoc in Tuchan. Katie Jones, the owner, specialises in small plots of, often forgotten, very old vines.

2016
Les perles de
JONES
CARIGNAN GRIS
VIEILLES VIGNES

Velouté froid de courgettes au chèvre frais – Chilled courgette and goat's cheese velouté

When it is hot and you really can't be bothered to cook or even eat, there is nothing better than chilled soup! It is great for the kids too; Louis, my son, and his best friend, Garance, can't get enough of this velouté served in fun little glasses or espresso cups!

Ingredients

- 4 green courgettes, washed and roughly diced
- 1 spring onion
- ½ small cucumber, peeled, seeds removed and roughly diced
- A handful of mixed fresh herbs – mint, basil and chives
- 100g fresh goat's cheese
- 500ml vegetable stock
- Salt and pepper to taste

Method

1. There are two methods to make this; the easy way or the really easy way!
2. The first way is to save back some herbs and goat's cheese for decoration and then put the rest into a blender with a handful of ice and blitz until smooth.
3. Check for seasoning, go easy with the salt as the goat's cheese is already salty, and sieve into a jug to remove the coarse fibres. Decant into a bottle with lid and chill.
4. The second method involves gently frying the courgettes and onion in olive oil for a couple of minutes and then cooking in stock until softened. The cooking process remove the sometimes harsh, sharpness of the onion and any bitterness in the courgettes.
5. Then put into the blender with the rest of the ingredients, saving back some herbs and cheese for the decoration.
6. Check for seasoning, and sieve into a jug to remove the coarse fibres. Decant into a bottle with a lid and chill.
7. Serve in chilled shot glasses with a crumbling of goat's cheese and a pinch of herbs.

Wine match

I usually serve this alongside the courgette carpaccio – a feast of courgettes. So this works well with the Perle Carignan Gris from Domaine Jones. However you could also try it with the elegant, aromatic and green fruited Chenin Blanc from Dutch/Irish winemakers Jan and Caryl Panman of Château Rives-Blanques in the Limoux hills. Theirs was the first ever 100% Chenin Blanc still wine in the Languedoc-Roussillon and has inspired many other producers.

Pesto aux fanes de radis - Radish leaf pesto

Ingredients

- 1 bunch of radish leaves (pick out any wilted or yellow leaves and discard)
- 1 large handful of fresh coriander
- 1 large handful of rocket
- 2 fresh garlic cloves
- 1 small spring onion
- The zest and juice of half a lemon
- 1 handful of whole almonds (with skins on)
- 1 to 2 tbsp roughly chopped or grated brebis cheese (the age and strength depends on your preference, I prefer a small quantity of sharp, tangy cheese)
- 1 to 2 tbsp quality olive oil (the best you have, as it really makes a difference)
- Seasoning to taste

This is best made in spring when the young radishes are in season and are plentiful at the market. You can use it as a dip, (just loosen it with more oil), as a salad dressing, on pasta, potatoes, drizzled onto fish or barbecued lamb, or as a base to a summer tomato tart. It is so versatile and if you make a big batch of it you can decant it into little pots and freeze it, otherwise it will keep in the fridge for the best part of a week.

Method

1. Wash the radish leaves thoroughly as they will probably be very gritty and spin dry in a salad spinner along with the rocket and coriander leaves.
2. Put into a food processor along with the garlic, spring onion, lemon zest and juice, almonds and cheese.
3. Blitz for several minutes and then drizzle in the olive oil until you have a paste-like consistency, scrape down and blitz again.
4. Taste and adjust the seasoning, you probably won't want any additional salt. Depending on the bitterness of the leaves add more, or less, brebis.
5. Alternatives: this is a very flexible pesto and can be adapted to whatever is in season. The key is to use the freshest of ingredients possible as any tiredness will be exaggerated in the final taste.
6. The rocket can be omitted or replaced with young spinach leaves. In the summer replace the coriander with basil and mint. Of course the almonds can be replaced with the more traditional pine nuts but they are not local to me here so are hugely expensive. Also I am very fearful of 'dysgeusia'* and what that might do to my palate and so tend to avoid them unless I am comfortable with the source,

Wine match

This will really depend on how you end up serving this pesto. However, it is very herby, slightly bitter and packs a tangy punch and so requires an aromatic wine with depth that won't be fazed, but equally won't try and fight with all those flavours. I would recommend it with Mas Champart's Indication Géographique Protégée (IGP) Pays D'Oc from Saint Chinian. A delicious blend of Terret (a local variety enjoying a come-back) and Grenache Gris, this is a rich, smooth wine with a mineral freshness.

* Dysgeusia refers to the persistent, unpleasant, and often metallic taste on the palate. It has been linked to pine nuts, especially those produced in China. It is a sensation that can last anything from a few hours to a lifetime. Hence my wariness!

Rillettes de truite – Coarse trout paté

Ingredients

- I large fresh trout fillet
- 200g smoked trout
- ¼ fennel bulb
- 1 small glass of white wine
- 1 tbsp freshly grated radish – here in the Languedoc we have plenty of piquant black radish, but horseradish would work equally well
- 2 tsp rinsed and chopped capers
- 2 tbsp salted butter, softened
- 2 tbsp crème fraîche
- 1 lemon, juice and zest finely grated
- 1 tbsp each of fresh chives and dill
- Salt and coarsely, ground pepper to taste

The streams here in the Languedoc-Roussillon are aplenty with fresh water trout. Trout is a delicate fish and requires careful handling. Rillette is a typically slow way of cooking in fat; here however the trout requires very little cooking and I have reduced the fat content by poaching in a wine and water bath. Traditionally it would be poached in duck, or goose, fat. If you would like to try the traditional way replace the liquid with 4 tbsp of fat and then do not add any butter later on. It will produce a richer rillette.

Method

1. Remove any bones left in the trout fillet with tweezers, rinse and pat dry.
2. Place the trout fillet in a large frying pan or wok with fennel, wine, pinch of salt and half the lemon. Cover with water and bring to a simmer then turn off the heat and leave to sit for five minutes.
3. Remove the trout from the pan and drain on some kitchen paper.
4. When cooled remove the skin and flake the trout into a bowl. Add the chopped smoked trout, capers, butter, the zest of the lemon, radish, crème fraîche and herbs. Mix well.
5. Check for seasoning and add lemon juice to taste.
6. The rillette should be of a coarse pate consistency.
7. Serve with hot toast and gherkins.

Wine match

A combination of richness from the butter and cream married with the delicate character of the trout requires an aromatic white with good acidity. Laurent Miquel of Casa Viel fame has planted in recent years the Albarino grape in his vineyards around the picturesque Corbières village of Lagrasse. Albarino is a variety that has found much fame and fortune in Galicia, Spain despite its French origin. It was taken to Galicia by the Cluny monks in the 12th century. Laurent's Albarino is full of crunchy green fruits, grapefruit and mineral.

Brandade de Nîmes – Salt cod from Nîmes

The majority of Brandade de Morue sold in the Languedoc is a very poor relation to the original dish which hails from the city of Nîmes. Today's versions found in all supermarkets and traiteurs tend to be more of a parmentier style, that is predominately mashed potatoes with the cod taking second place! The original recipe as you will see below has no potato and is a delicate dish lightly flavoured with olive oil, white pepper and nutmeg. It was traditionally invented by the cook of the Archbishop of Arlès, the term brandade comes from the Occitan 'brandar' meaning to stir, or shake, vigorously. There is a school of thought that you should not add the garlic to the final blend; personally I think it benefits the dish, but that is your choice!

Ingredients

- 1 kg salt cod
- 300ml quality olive oil, warmed to blood temperature
- 240ml milk, warmed to blood temperature
- 2 large cloves of garlic
- 2 bay leaves
- White pepper
- Nutmeg
- Juice of 1 lemon
- Chopped parsley to serve

Method

1. Start this recipe at least three days before you want to eat it as the salt cod needs a good 24–48 hours of soaking.
2. Rinse the salt cod under the cold tap to remove the salt, then place into a container with a lid with plenty of fresh water. Pop in the fridge and remember to change the water three times a day, rinsing the cod at each change.
3. On the third day remove the cod from the fridge and rinse a last time. Then place into a large saucepan with plenty of fresh, cold water, the bay leaves, garlic cloves and half a lemon.
4. Heat the cod but watch like a hawk as you want to remove it from the heat just before it starts to boil, roughly 8 minutes. It is important that it doesn't boil as this would make the cod very tough and chewy.
5. Remove from the water, drain and cool in a colander. Keep the garlic cloves, but throw the rest.
6. Once cool enough to handle pick through the fish removing any bones, skin or scum that might have formed. Whilst you are doing this you can be gently heating the oil and milk, in separate pans.
7. Traditionally they would do the next part by hand beating firmly with a wooden spoon. I confess I take the modern lazy option of using a food processor. You can choose to be traditional if you have the time and muscles! Place the fish, the cooked garlic (if using, I suggest adding one and then tasting for strength before adding the second; it shouldn't dominate the flavour of the cod), a small pinch of white pepper and nutmeg to the food processor and mix on a gentle setting.
8. Slowly trickle in the warmed oil and milk, alternating between one and the other until a creamy consistency has formed. You may not need all of the milk and oil, however if you are not eating immediately you will find that the mixture solidifies in the fridge and so will need loosening with more oil or milk.
9. Taste for seasoning and adjust the pepper and nutmeg accordingly, you shouldn't need to add any salt. A squeeze of lemon will add a freshness and stir through some freshly, chopped parsley.
10. This can be served with garlic toasts, as a dip, stuffed into roasted vegetables such as peppers or courgettes.

Wine match

The pungency of the oil, the salty, yet delicateness of the cod, combined with garlic, white pepper and nutmeg demands a Mediterranean white wine with some complexity. I have tried many wines over the years, and enjoyed the match, but I think one of the best matches was from Olivier Pithon, another stunning domaine in the tiny village of Calces. His D18, (named after the road that runs through Calce), is a complex blend of Grenache Gris and Blanc. Barrel aged for 12 months this wine benefits from decanting. Serve only lightly chilled.

Accras de morue - Salt cod balls

These little fish balls are very moreish; one is never enough, so best to make a big batch. They freeze well and although anything deep-fried is always best served immediately, you can fry these in advance and then reheat in the oven if you want to get ahead. I have adapted this recipe from one I found on the Food and Wine website: www.foodandwine.com.

Ingredients

- 500g salt cold
- 500g potatoes, use a good potato for mashing
- 250ml milk
- 2 bay leaves
- A sprig of thyme
- 3 garlic cloves
- 2 spring onions, finely chopped
- 1 tsp piment d'espelette
- 1 tsp smoked paprika
- 1 lemon, juice and zest
- 1 to 2 tbsp finely chopped parsley
- Pinch of white pepper
- 4 eggs
- Flour for coating
- Roughly 200g breadcrumbs. I use an 80/20 mix of breadcrumbs and polenta to give a nice crunchy texture

Method

1. First rinse and then soak the cod. Change the water at least three times a day, for at least two days.
2. Then rinse the cod a final time and put it into a pan with the bay leaves, garlic cloves, thyme and milk. Cover with enough water so that everything is fully submerged.
3. Simmer, without boiling, for 20 minutes.
4. Remove the fish with a slotted spoon and cool. When cool, remove and discard any bones and skin, flake the flesh into a bowl and set aside.
5. Peel and roughly cube the potatoes, cook in the milky fish stock until soft. Remove from the pan with a slotted spoon and mash with the poached garlic and enough of the milky stock to create a loose mash.
6. Add the spring onion, parsley, lemon zest and juice, pepper, paprika and piment to the mash and stir vigorously.
7. Add two egg yolks and the fish, mixing until everything is thoroughly combined. Taste it; you shouldn't need to add any salt, if you find it to too salty then add more lemon juice.
8. Cover and put into the fridge until you are ready to serve.
9. Before rolling the balls it is best to get all your ingredients and equipment to hand as this is the messy part!
10. Prepare a clean surface. Get a couple of baking sheets ready lined with paper to put the fish balls on. Have a plate for the flour to dredge the balls in, a shallow bowl with the beaten eggs (you can add the extra egg whites here or if you prefer keep them back to make meringues) and another for the breadcrumb and polenta mix. It is also wise to have a large bowl of cold water and a towel to rinse your hands from time to time.
11. Get the fish mix out of the fridge and with clean, wet hands proceed to roll the balls to roughly 2cm in diameter. It doesn't really matter, make them as big or as small as you like, just adjust the cooking time accordingly.
12. I find that I can do about half a dozen at a time, then dredge in flour, eggs and breadcrumbs.
13. Put directly onto the baking sheet and repeat, cleaning your hands as you go and always rolling the balls with wet hands to stop the mix sticking too much.
14. It's a messy job, and if you doubled up the recipe as I do, be prepared to ignore the phone, the door, requests to help with Lego for a good half hour!
15. Once done put into the fridge to firm up, at least an hour.
16. When ready to cook get your deep fat fryer set up with clean vegetable oil, a slotted spoon to take the balls out with, plenty of kitchen roll to drain them on and a serving dish. If you are serving immediately it is a good idea to turn the oven onto a low heat so that you can keep the cooked balls warm whilst you fry the rest.
17. Heat the oil and fry the balls in batches, turning them as they cook. They are done when they are a pleasing brown colour all over. I suggest you cook one first and taste it to get the feel of it.
18. Serve hot with plenty of fresh lemon.

Wine match

These salty little balls have an element of spice from the piment and a grassy character from the spring onions and parsley. They work very well with the Domaine Mouscaillo white, a Chardonnay dominant wine from the Limoux hills in the tiny village of Roquetaillade. Pierre and Marie-Claire Fort produce just three wines and have only 5ha of vineyard. Their wines are fine examples of terroir and grape variety, elegant and finely crafted. This is an intensely mineral style, think of Chablis, and is one of the best Chardonnays that the region produces. A wine to be enjoyed both in its youth but also for the long term.

Gazpacho - Chilled tomato soup

This is only worth making in the height of summer when the tomatoes are bursting with ripeness and flavour. Serve chilled, it is pure heaven on a hot summer's day. A good friend in the village, a vigneron, had a terrible accident which left him without any taste sensation and only able to eat liquids through a straw. As you can imagine he was very depressed. I made him some of this gazpacho to cheer him up and it revitalised his palate and restored his good humour. Life changing gazpacho! Serve in shot glasses

Ingredients

- 1 kg of very ripe tomatoes, stalks removed and roughly chopped
- 1 red pepper, seeded, pith removed and roughly chopped
- 1 red spring onion, here we get delicious large red spring onions you can replace with a normal red onion if you can't get these where you are
- 2 large garlic cloves
- ½ small cucumber, peeled if the skin is tough
- 1 large handful of fresh basil
- 2 tbsp sherry vinegar
- Olive oil
- Salt and pepper
- Ice and water

Method

1. You will need a good blender, a sieve and some patience but otherwise this is such an easy recipe.
2. Wash and roughly chop all the vegetables, make sure you remove any bad bits as they will be noticed in the final soup.
3. Pop into the blender and blitz.
4. Add the vinegar, oil, seasoning, basil and salt and pepper (you will need a good pinch of salt as you tend to need more salt when serving things chilled. Blitz again
5. Add a handful of ice and water to loosen it, blitz and taste.
6. Adjust seasoning and vinegar to suit your palate.
7. When you are happy with the flavour sieve the soup into a jug. This is a slow process but essential, there is something about the sieving and removing of the fibrous parts of the vegetables that brings out the aromatics and makes the gazpacho 'sing'. Leave this stage out and you will regret it! I do this first thing in the morning, multi tasking, alternately letting the soup filter on its own and pushing it through with a wooden spoon.
8. You can usually add another glass of cold water through the mashed veg in the sieve and not lose any flavour.
9. Once done decant into a bottle; a cleaned out juice bottle works well, and refrigerate.
10. Serve in small glasses, I have a stack of glass yoghurt pots that work well. Serve with a swirl of punchy olive oil and a basil leaf. It is traditional to add a teaspoon of chopped vegetables, a combination of tomato, red pepper, cucumber and avocado. Sometimes I do, sometimes I don't. Often I find just sipping it as is without anything in the way or the need for cutlery, rather delightful.
11. A variation would be to add some raw beetroot this would increase the sweetness so to keep the tangy element increase the vinegar.

Wine match

Soups are often rather hard to match, liquids and liquids, just too many liquids! And this liquid salad has the added complexity of vinegar –wine's nemesis! However we have over the years enjoyed it with a glass of the delicious Mescladis from Pierre Clavel. A Syrah based rosé grown in the dramatic vineyards of Pic St Loup, in the north of the Languedoc. Crunchy raspberry and redcurrant fruits abound, fruity and refreshing. Serve chilled.

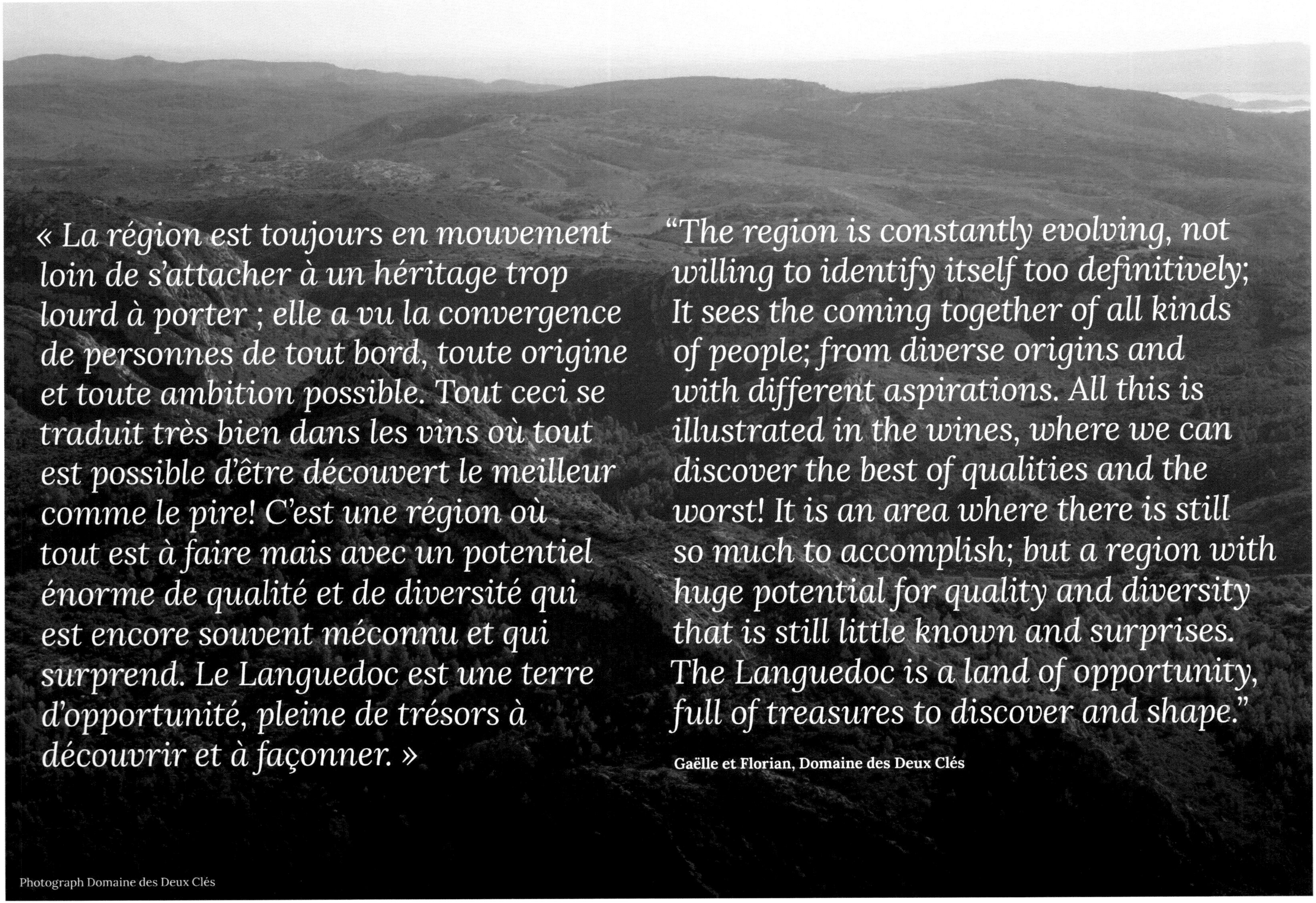

« La région est toujours en mouvement loin de s'attacher à un héritage trop lourd à porter ; elle a vu la convergence de personnes de tout bord, toute origine et toute ambition possible. Tout ceci se traduit très bien dans les vins où tout est possible d'être découvert le meilleur comme le pire! C'est une région où tout est à faire mais avec un potentiel énorme de qualité et de diversité qui est encore souvent méconnu et qui surprend. Le Languedoc est une terre d'opportunité, pleine de trésors à découvrir et à façonner. »

"The region is constantly evolving, not willing to identify itself too definitively; It sees the coming together of all kinds of people; from diverse origins and with different aspirations. All this is illustrated in the wines, where we can discover the best of qualities and the worst! It is an area where there is still so much to accomplish; but a region with huge potential for quality and diversity that is still little known and surprises. The Languedoc is a land of opportunity, full of treasures to discover and shape."

Gaëlle et Florian, Domaine des Deux Clés

Photograph Domaine des Deux Clés

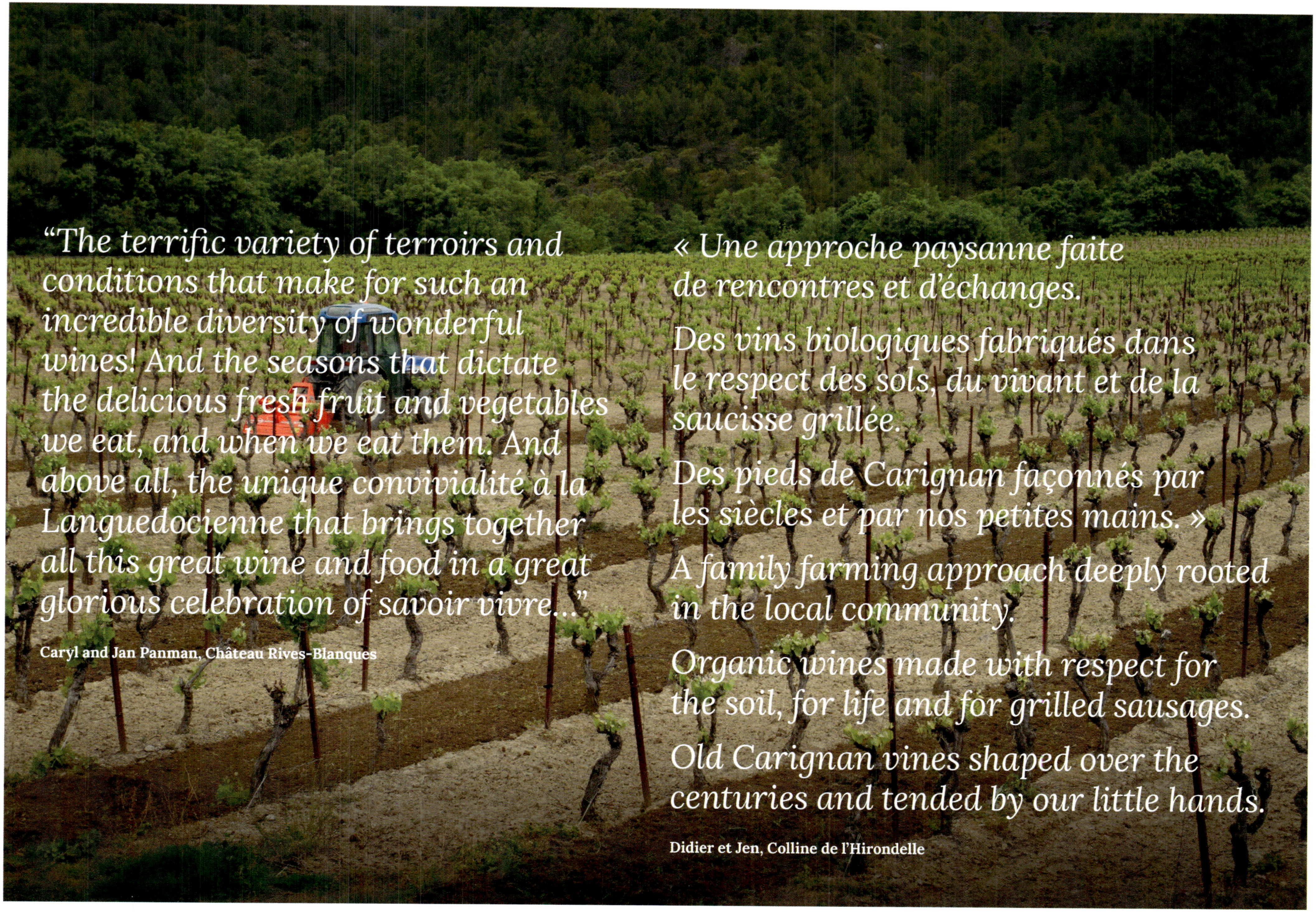

"The terrific variety of terroirs and conditions that make for such an incredible diversity of wonderful wines! And the seasons that dictate the delicious fresh fruit and vegetables we eat, and when we eat them. And above all, the unique convivialité à la Languedocienne that brings together all this great wine and food in a great glorious celebration of savoir vivre..."

Caryl and Jan Panman, Château Rives-Blanques

« Une approche paysanne faite de rencontres et d'échanges.

Des vins biologiques fabriqués dans le respect des sols, du vivant et de la saucisse grillée.

Des pieds de Carignan façonnés par les siècles et par nos petites mains. »

A family farming approach deeply rooted in the local community.

Organic wines made with respect for the soil, for life and for grilled sausages.

Old Carignan vines shaped over the centuries and tended by our little hands.

Didier et Jen, Colline de l'Hirondelle

Caviar d'aubergine - Aubergine purée

I have put these two dishes together as I often serve them together at home, although I don't tend to use the Baba at tastings as it is not from this region. The caviar is and is always popular even with those that don't normally like aubergines.

Ingredients

- 2 large aubergines
- 1 red pepper
- 1 small courgette
- 1 red onion
- 3 garlic cloves
- 1 tsp ground cumin powder
- 1 tbsp Herbs de Provence
- Sea salt and cracked black pepper
- Plenty of good quality olive oil

Method

1. Heat the oven to 150°C, pop one of the aubergines onto the diffuser over the gas hob and cook until the skin is blackened and the flesh soft, turning from time to time with tongs.
2. Remove from the heat and leave to cool in a bowl, drain off the juices.
3. Meanwhile finely dice all of the remaining vegetables and put into an oven proof dish with the cumin, herbs, seasoning and plenty of olive oil.
4. Slowly roast, stirring from time to time and adding more olive oil if necessary. Don't overdo the oil however as the aubergines will release oil when cooked and cooled.
5. If you find that the caviar is cooking too quickly turn down the heat because the aim is to slowly roast the vegetables to get that rich, opulent, confit flavour.
6. Remove from the oven and cool.
7. Peel the smoked aubergine and mash the flesh, add to the caviar.
8. At this point you can decide to either keep the caviar as is, or to purée it and serve as a dip. If I am serving it at the same time as the Baba I tend to leave it as chopped veg to add a contrast.
9. Serve with bread and crudités.

Baba ghanoush

This is a middle Eastern dish made with aubergine. There are many variations to this recipe but I was taught how to prepare it by an Arabian friend and it is delicious and never fails to impress. There are two key elements to this recipe which makes it stand out from any other baba ghanoush that I have tried. Firstly, the diffuser, by cooking the aubergines on this you get a rich smoky character which is reminiscent of cooking on ashes as they would have traditionally done. You can roast the aubergines in an oven but it doesn't taste the same at all. Secondly, by doing everything by hand instead of whizzing up in a mixer you get a coarser but more flavoursome dish rather than a goopy purée!

Ingredients

- 2 large firm aubergine
- 2 to 3 plump garlic cloves
- 1 tsp rock salt
- 1 tbsp tahini paste (sesame purée)
- 1 lemon
- 2 tsp cumin seeds
- 1 tsp smoked paprika
- Cayenne pepper (optional)

Method

This is a recipe to adapt to your own personal taste so play around with quantities until you are happy, but the final product should be smoky and garlicky with an Eastern kick.

1. Take the diffuser (you can get these at any cookware or hardware store and they only cost a couple of Euros so are worth the investment) and put it directly onto the hob.
2. Pop the two washed, whole aubergines on and let them cook. The aubergines will need turning but otherwise you can leave them to do their business whilst you do something else. They are ready when the skins are black all over and the aubergine is soft to touch.
3. Once ready remove with tongs and put in a bowl until cool enough to handle. When cool gently peel off the skin; it should come off easily in flakes. Remove the stalk and mash the aubergine with a fork. If cooked properly this is easily done. If a lot of juice has come off the aubergine, strain before mashing.
4. In a pestle and mortar pound the garlic cloves with a large pinch of sea salt. The salt acts as a grip to the garlic whilst also seasoning the dish. When you have a garlic paste add to the aubergine mix.
5. Now add the tahini. As these come in different strengths it is best to start with a large teaspoon and then add more if needed. Some brands can be very strong; I recommend a good organic one.
6. Squeeze the juice of half a lemon and add (again more can be added if needed at the end).
7. In a small pan dry fry the cumin seeds. This releases all their pungent aromas. It only takes a few seconds so do keep shaking the pan and tossing the seeds; beware as they can burn easily! Pound these in the pestle and mortar and add to the aubergine mix along with a large pinch of paprika and a hint of cayenne (optional if you like a kick or not).
8. Mix well and taste. If it is too solid you can add some olive oil and more lemon juice. I sometimes add chopped coriander.
9. Serve at room temperature with toasted flat breads and crudités.

Wine match

This is often served as part of a meze and so matching each dish on its own is rather pointless as there would be numerous dishes on offer and usually only one or two wines. Aubergines however are very wine friendly vegetables and complement a variety of wines. I find that the smoky character in both these dishes, the piquancy of the garlic in the Baba and the herbiness in the caviar work well with a red wine with very little oak (the cumin makes oak taste bitter) but plenty of 'garrigue' character. Domaine de L'Hortus, in the dramatic district of the Pic St Loup produce a fabulous red; their Bergerie de L'Hortus is a Mourvèdre based wine blended with Syrah and Grenache, plenty of crunchy black fruits and smoked herbs, serve cool, not cold.

Empanadillas au Thon – Spicy Tuna pastries

Ingredients

- 425g of dolphin friendly tuna
- 1 small red onion, finely chopped
- 2 cloves of garlic, finely chopped
- ½ red and ½ green bell pepper, diced
- 1 tbsp capers, chopped
- 2 tablespoons mixed green and black olives, pitted and chopped
- 1 tbsp each of freshly chopped parsley and oregano
- 1 tsp paprika
- Large pinch Piment d'Espelette
- Salt and pepper to taste
- 2 tbsp olive oil
- Lemon juice to taste

Pastry

- 300g plain flour
- 150g cold butter cut into cubes (I use salted then I don't need to add extra later on)
- 1 egg + 1 more for the egg wash
- 1 small glass of ice cold water

Method

1. First make the pastry: put the flour and butter into a food processor and pulse.
2. Add the egg and a little bit of water, pulse. Add more water if required.
3. Once the dough has come together knead gently on a floured surface then roll into a ball, cover with cling film and put into a cool place.
4. Whilst the dough is resting make the filling.
5. Heat one tbsp of the oil and gently fry the onion until soft, add the garlic and bell peppers and cook for a further five minutes.
6. Add the capers, olives, herbs, paprika and piment, stir until combined. Remove from the heat, check the seasoning, and add more oil if it looks dry and a squeeze of lemon juice to taste.
7. Set aside to cool. Note the filling can be made the day before and kept chilled in the fridge.
8. Heat the oven to 200°C and line two baking trays with greaseproof paper and generously flour your work surface.
9. Unwrap the dough, knead it and roll out to roughly 2mm and cut out round shapes using a saucer as a guide, around 10cm diameter.
10. Put a teaspoon of stuffing in the middle then fold over the pastry and firmly press the edges to seal. If you find that they do not seal easily try brushing the inside edges with some egg white or water to act as a glue. Try not to over fill, as you will find it hard to seal the empanadillas properly and they will leak when cooking.
11. At this point you can either crimp the edges with your fingers, use a fork (easier) or if you are feeling adventurous, make a churito, the traditional curl type seal, using your fingers to twist the edges. I suggest you take a look at www.laylita.com for an informative video guide on how to make empanada dough.
12. Place onto your baking sheet and brush with a beaten egg to ensure a golden finish.
13. Pop into the fridge for half an hour before baking so that they firm up.
14. Then bake for 18–25 minutes, checking them after fifteen minutes as the cooking time will depend on the size that you end up making.
15. Remove and cool on a wire rack. Serve warm or cold.

Wine match

Tuna and rosé are a match made in heaven, however there are plenty of bold flavours here so a Provence rosé style wine would be too light in style to cope. Château La Voulte Gasparets does a super rosé full of flavour, red fruits, garrigue and mineral. Made in the saignée method, a blend of Grenache, Mourvèdre and Carignan. Serve chilled but not cold, at around 12–13°C.

Tielle Sétoise
- Octopus and tomato pies from Sète

These little octopus pies come from the pretty town of Sète, sometimes called the Venice of the Languedoc due to the canals that run though the town. The pies were created by the Italian fish-wives for their husbands when they went out to sea. I once took a group of clients on a weekend gastronomic tour in and around Sète and they fell in love with these tielles and named them octo-pies, and the name has stuck since! They are rather fiddly to make but the difference between the home-made version and shop bought is worth that effort. I have experimented with all sorts of crust and have come to the conclusion that this simple olive oil crust works best, as a dough is, well, too doughy to be honest. The addition of polenta gives a pleasing crunch.

Ingredients

- 500g octopus, or squid tubes
- 1 medium onion finely chopped
- 3 cloves garlic, finely chopped
- Saffron, large pinch
- 1 tsp piment d'espelette
- 4 large tomatoes, peeled, seeded and diced or 1 tin of puréed tomatoes
- 1 tbsp tomato purée
- 1 tbsp fresh rosemary finely chopped
- 2 tbsp olive oil
- Salt and pepper to taste
- Pastry:
- 450g strong plain flour
- 100g fine polenta
- 1 tbsp tomato purée
- 4 tbsp olive oil
- 10 ml Muscat de Frontignan
- Pinch of salt
- Cold water

Method

1. If you are using octopus it is best to freeze it first as this ensures that it is tender, so you need to buy it several days before you want to make these. The day before, remove from the freezer and defrost thoroughly, then bring a large pan of water to boil with some bay leaves, half a lemon, coriander seeds, whole garlic cloves and a large glug of olive oil. With a pair of tongs plunge the octopus into the boiling water and pull out, plunge again and pull out with the tongs, repeat three times. This ensures that the tentacles curl up nicely and that the meat tenderises. Then submerge the octopus into the water, ensure that it is covered completely, and simmer for 30 to 40 minutes until you can pierce it with a fork easily. Drain and cool.
2. To make the pastry put all of the ingredients (except the water) into a food processor and combine, slowly add enough ice cold water to form a ball. Remove, knead gently on a floured surface then wrap and rest it in the fridge whilst you make the stuffing.
3. In a heavy bottomed frying pan heat the oil with a pinch of salt, add the onions so they soften but remain translucent but if they start to colour turn down the heat.
4. Add the garlic, the saffron, rosemary and piment. Stir well to combine
5. Now add the octopus, cut into fine dice (or squid tubes cut into fine rings)
6. Add the tomatoes and purée, a few grinds of pepper and simmer on a gentle heat until thickened. Check for seasoning. Then cool.
7. Heat the oven to 180°C, prepare your mould, you can either make one large tielle or several small ones. For my tastings I always make the small ones and this usually yields around 24. Generously oil two muffin cases with twelve holes.
8. On a well-floured, cool surface roll out the pastry to roughly 3mm thickness and cut out the circles to suit your muffin tin, mine are 5cm in diameter, saving enough pastry for the lids which should be slightly smaller.
9. Fill the pies with the stuffing, roughly a dessert spoon's worth, making sure that you drain off any liquid.
10. Brush the edges of the lid and 'glue' onto the base. There is a traditional way of sealing the edges of a tielle: using a knife, make 2 to 3cm incisions all around the edge of the pie, every 2cm, then pinch in the strips of pastry.
11. Brush the pies either with olive oil or if there is any sauce left over with some of the tomato sauce and cook for 15 to 20 minutes until the pies take on an orange colour.
12. Remove from the oven and cool. Serve either cold or warm.

Wine match

These spicy tomato and octopus pies work so well with a full flavoured rosé. Fifteen minutes down the road from me here in the Corbières is a small Domaine owned by husband and wife team Didier and Jen of the Colline de L'Hirondelle. They produce quirky, hand crafted wines, small in quantity and large in flavour. Their rosé, Ventilo, is made from the much forgotten, and dismissed, Chenançon variety. The ripeness of the fruit here ensures that the wine harmonises, rather than is overpowered by the spiciness of the sauce; just don't serve it too cold!

Salade de lentilles vertes – Green lentil salad

This is a delicious combination of earthy and nutty lentils, fresh herbs and salty lardons. You can replace coriander with basil in the summer and the lardons with toasted walnuts to make it vegetarian.

Ingredients

- 250g Lauragais or Puy lentils
- 2 bay leaves
- 2 large garlic cloves
- 2 red spring onions, finely chopped
- 200g lardons
- 1 handful of fresh parsley, coriander and chives, chopped
- A handful of sliced cherry tomatoes if in season, otherwise you could use a few sun-dried tomatoes but reduce the salt in the dressing

Dressing

- 4tbsp olive oil
- 2tsp red wine vinegar
- 1 heaped tsp of Dijon mustard
- Salt and pepper to taste

Method

1. Start by cooking the lentils. Rinse thoroughly and check for stones. Put in a large pan with cold water, salt, one of the garlic cloves (peeled and whole) and the bay leaves.
2. Bring to the boil and simmer for 10 minutes then turn off the heat and allow to sit for approximately five more minutes. Be careful not to overcook, you want the lentils to be just al dente.
3. Drain. Pick out and discard the garlic and bay leaves. Rinse the lentils thoroughly under cold water.
4. In a frying pan cook the lardons until crispy. You probably won't need to add any additional oil as they tend to be quite fatty.
5. Add the remaining garlic clove (finely chopped) to the pan for the last couple of minutes to just soften, but not brown.
6. Mix together the ingredients for the dressing, taste and put aside.
7. In a large salad bowl mix together the lentils, the spring onions, lardons and garlic, tomatoes (if using) and herbs.
8. Half an hour before serving add the dressing and mix well. Check for seasoning and leave to infuse.

Wine match

The earthy, herby flavours of this salad are very wine friendly and match well with a herby red wine full of the garrigue characteristics found here in the Corbières. My neighbouring village, Fontjoncouse, is home to an exciting new domaine called Domaine des Deux Clés. Owned by a French and German young couple, they are producing small quantities of high quality wines. For this dish I chose their Corbières Rouge; an aromatic, vibrant red full of pepper and spice and a hint of menthol freshness. I recommend serving it on the cooler side, 14/15°C.

Patatas Espagnoles - Spanish potatoes

These potatoes are very easy to make and can be served as a tapas dish on its own or be part of a main meal. Replace the chorizo with charred red peppers to make it vegetarian.

Ingredients

- 1kg of new potatoes
- 1 head of garlic
- 4 tbsp tomato purée
- 1 tbsp smoked paprika
- 200g spicy chorizo
- 1 lemon
- 1 tbsp rosemary, finely chopped
- 3 to 4 tbsp olive oil
- Salt and pepper

Method

1. Heat the oven to 180C.
2. Wash the potatoes. Cut any large ones in half as you are looking to make bite sized pieces.
3. In a bowl mix together the tomato purée, paprika, lemon juice, olive oil, rosemary and seasoning.
4. Add the potatoes and mix well.
5. Chop the chorizo into half-moons 2mm thick. Separate the garlic cloves and smash with the back of a knife, this makes it much easier to peel off the skin. It is fashionable to leave the skins on, but whilst it might stop the garlic from burning, I find that the skin is an unwanted addition and a faff to remove at the end of the cooking process.
6. In a wide, oven proof dish add the potatoes, garlic and chorizo. Mix so that everything is coated in the sauce.
7. Cook in the oven for 25 minutes, stirring from time to time and adding extra oil if needed. Adjust the heat if you feel that the garlic is cooking too fast.
8. Check the seasoning and serve drizzled with olive oil.

Wine match

This is more of an accompaniment than a stand-alone dish so it will depend on what else is being served. That said, the key elements here are the smoked paprika and the spice from the chorizo, so a chilled red is the best choice. Domaine de la Rune in Talairan produce a lively, crisp red called Wunjo. Unusually this is made from 100% Cinsault, a grape usually found in blends. This wine is packed with crunchy red fruits and works well with the spice here.

There seem to be as many versions of Zarzuela out there as there are days in the year! I am sure that they are all tasty but not necessarily authentic, and I am about to add to that collection with my version. All I can say is that it is hugely popular.

Ingredients

- 2 fillets of firm white fish (choose from monkfish, sea bream, hake, blue ling)
- 2 medium cuttlefish (cleaned, the bodies cut into rings and the tentacles chopped)
- 1 large handful each of mussels, clams and prawns
- 1 small fennel bulb finely diced
- 1 medium onion finely diced
- 2 large garlic cloves diced, plus an extra for rubbing on the toast
- 1 red pepper finely diced
- 4 large tomatoes, peeled, seeded and diced (or 1 tin chopped tomatoes)
- 1 tbsp tomato purée
- 175ml fish stock *
- Large pinch of saffron
- Paprika to taste
- 1 large handful of fresh, chopped parsley plus extra for serving
- 1 tbsp of Pastis (an aromatic aniseed spirit)
- 1 small glass of white wine
- Salt and pepper to taste
- Olive oil for frying and drizzling on the toasts
- Bread to make garlic toasts

Method

1. If you have bought the cuttlefish fresh, which I strongly advise you to do, you will need to deal with this first as this is the messiest part! Remove the heads and clean out the body under cold water, chop the tentacles and add to a bowl of cold water with the bodies and let them soak for as long as possible to remove any sand. Drain, rinse and drain again before using.
2. Equally rinse and soak the mussels and clams and soak in cold water until you are ready for them, then drain and rinse and drain again.
3. Next chop all your vegetables so that they are ready.
4. Choose a heavy bottomed pan with a lid that you are happy to bring to the table as this is a dip-in and share sort of a dish.
5. Start by adding a couple of tablespoons of olive oil to the pan on a medium heat, then add the cuttlefish rings (keep the tentacles aside for now), cook for 2 to 3 minutes until translucent. Remove from the pan with a slotted spoon and keep aside for later
6. Add more oil to the pan if needed and a small pinch of salt and the onions. Soften for 2 to 3 minutes.
7. Now add the fennel, pepper, garlic, paprika and saffron. Cook for a further five minutes.
8. Pour the Pastis over and stir. After about five minutes the alcohol will have burned off and you are left with an aromatic aniseed aroma.
9. Now add the tomatoes and purée, stir well and cook for another five minutes.
10. Add the wine and stock. You may not need all of the stock at this point so hold some back to add later on, especially if you are making this in advance and then reheating. Cook for 10 to 15 minutes until the liquid has reduced and the sauce thickened.
11. Add the fish, parsley and black pepper.
12. Lower the heat, put the lid on and cook gently for five minutes.
13. If you are doing this in advance turn the heat off now and put aside.
14. Otherwise now add the rest of the seafood, mussels, cuttlefish rings and tentacles, prawns and clams. Cook until the shells open.
15. Check the seasoning at this point, the seafood is naturally salty so you may not need to add any extra salt. If the sauce has thickened too much loosen it with some of the reserved fish stock.
16. Sprinkle with parsley and serve with garlic croutons. I also sometimes serve with a mix of garlic croutons, tapenade and radish leaf pesto.

Wine match

This dish works equally well with a robust white or a full flavoured rosé. For the white I recommend Domaine de la Rectorie's L'Argile, an elegant Grenache Gris dominated wine, with notes of fennel and white fruits, mineral and sea salt. Alternatively Domaine Ollier Taillefer do a delicious rosé, Les Collines. A blend of Grenache, Syrah and Mourvèdre, lightly spicy and again the wafts of fennel work very well indeed here.

* Fish stock – you can make your own using the prawn shells and any bones/heads from the fish, just throw it all into a pan with cold water, a glass of wine, parsley stalks, an onion, carrot and the parts of the fennel that you would normally throw away. Cook on a medium heat whilst you prepare the rest of the Zarzuela.

Zarzuela - Catalan fish stew

Encornets farcis - Stuffed cuttlefish

Ingredients

- 8 cuttlefish, (the size can really vary so you may find that 1 per person is enough or that you need 2 or 3 each)
- 1 onion, finely diced
- 3 cloves of garlic, diced
- 1 carrot, peeled and finely diced
- 1 small fennel, diced
- 300g sausage meat (or a mix of sausage and minced veal)
- 1 tin chopped tomatoes
- 1 tbsp tomato purée
- 1 tbsp Herbs de Provence
- 1 bay leaf
- 1 tsp piment d'espelette
- 1 glass of white wine
- Olive oil to fry
- Salt and pepper

You see huge pans in the market at Lezignan filled with these little squids, the aroma filling the air and whetting the appetite. Serve with a mix of plain and wild rice from the Camargue, which adds a nice nutty texture.

Method

1. Start by cleaning out the cuttlefish, or ask the fishmonger to do this. Otherwise empty the sac, remove the centre bone and rinse thoroughly under cold water. Rinse the sand off from the tentacles and chop into 1cm pieces. Set aside in a bowl of cold water until you are ready to use.
2. In a large heavy bottomed frying pan or wok with lid, gently fry the onion until softened but not coloured.
3. Add the rest of the vegetables and cook for 5 to 10 minutes until softened.
4. Add the tentacles and the sausage meat, breaking it up with the spoon.
5. Once the meat has started to lightly brown add the herbs, piment, tomatoes, tomato purée and wine. Combine.
6. Season, turn down the heat and simmer with a lid on until the sauce thickens.
7. Turn off the heat and allow to cool.
8. Check the seasoning and stuff the squids with the mixture, putting any extra sauce around and onto the encornets. If the sauce is too thick loosen with a splash of water.
9. Place in an ovenproof dish that you can bring to the table and cook at 200°C for half an hour until the squids are easily pierced with a knife.
10. If you have a sharp knife it is nice to serve these sliced and spread out like a fan on a bed of rice with plenty of sauce.

Wine match

This is the sort of dish that you can serve with any colour of wine, it is that adaptable! White, rosé or red (low in tannins and oak) would all work. I served it with Tom Lubb's white from Domaine Matassa from the Roussillon village of Calce, a small place with an extraordinary number of high quality winemakers and wines. This is a superb, age-worthy wine made from Grenache Gris (70%) and Macabeu (30%) in accordance with biodynamic principals. Decant and serve only lightly chilled. The flavours are nutty, with layers of garrigue herbs, hints of pear and a slightly salty finish. A very interesting wine.

This method of cooking fish works equally well with either a swordfish steak or squid tubes*. It is a very simple dish, in both the preparation and the cooking method, which means that the quality of the fish is paramount. Use the freshest that you can. One tuna steak can serve two as a main course served warm with a potato and asparagus salad or it can be chopped into bite sized cubes to share as a tapas dish with the radish leaf pesto on the side.

Ingredients

- 1 large tuna steak, roughly 3 cm in thickness
- 2 tbsp fruity olive oil such as a Picholine oil
- 1/2 tsp wasabi paste
- Plenty of freshly cracked pepper
- Juice of ½ a lime
- Rock salt to taste

Method

1. In a small bowl mix together the oil, juice, pepper, salt and wasabi.
2. Place the tuna in a wide, flat dish and cover with the marinade. Rub the marinade into the fish so that it is evenly coated.
3. Cover and refrigerate, for at least two hours or overnight.
4. Half an hour before you are ready to cook remove from the fridge and bring up to room temperature.
5. Heat a griddle pan until it is very hot and place the tuna on it There is no need for any more oil as there is enough in the marinade.
6. Leave it to sear, depending on the thickness of the fish and whether you have heated the griddle hot enough this should take about 2 to 3 minutes. It may be tempting at this point to poke the fish and try to flip it over too soon but if you do it will stick to the griddle pan and break up. Patience is a virtue and you will be rewarded with a perfectly sealed piece of tuna.
7. Flip and seal the other side.
8. The fish should have a pleasing griddle imprint on each side, yet be very rare inside, treat it like you would a rump steak. If you overcook tuna it dries out and the resulting fish is crumbly and tasteless. An expensive mistake.
9. Place the fish onto a board to rest, drizzle with more olive oil and squeeze of lime and some cracked black pepper.

Wine match

This works with any of the rosés that I have already mentioned in this book, but for an unusual combination why not try a lightly chilled glass of red. There is a small domaine near the salt marshes of Gruissan, Domaine d'Ile St Martin that produces a Vin de France made from 100% Piquepoul Noir. This is a little known grape variety found in the Languedoc-Roussillon. Here it makes a light red wine, in both colour and alcohol, that is fruity and peppery with soft, approachable tannins. Serve lightly chilled.

* Both these fishes would be better matched with a dry rosé or a full bodied white wine rather than the red that I have recommended for the tuna

Thon à la plancha - Chargrilled tuna

Brochette de lotte au romarin – Rosemary monkfish skewers

We barbecue a lot in the south as the last place you want to be on a hot day is inside, cooking. However not everyone has access to a barbecue so if that is the case for you I recommend investing in a decent plancha as that is as close as you can get to an indoor barbecue. In Spain they sell double sided planchas for as little as 20€. If monkfish is not sustainable in the area where you are replace it with any firm, white fleshed fish.

Ingredients

- 2 medium sized monkfish tails roughly 650g in weight
- 3 to 4 sprigs of rosemary, removed from the wood and chopped finely
- 1 lemon; juice and zest
- 2 tbsp of flavoursome olive oil
- Sea salt and cracked black pepper to taste

Method

1. Remove the centre bone from the monkfish tails and any skin. Put the bone aside to use for a stock (if you have no need of the stock right away you can freeze these for another day).
2. With a very sharp knife cut the monkfish into 2 to 3cm cubes, skewer a hole into the middle of each piece.
3. Place into a bowl and add the rosemary, lemon zest, olive oil and seasoning. Cover and refrigerate.
4. Leave to marinate for at least two hours.
5. If you have lots of rosemary it is fun to make the skewers from rosemary wood, otherwise use wooden skewers soaked in water.
6. Thread the fish onto the skewers, 3 to 4 pieces each.
7. Barbecue on a medium light heat grill for roughly two minutes on each side, brushing with the rosemary oil as you go.
8. Don't overcook or the fish will dry out, it should be lightly browned on the outside. Remember that it will continue to cook even when you remove it from the heat.
9. This can be served on its own as a tapas or with a green salad and Spanish potatoes.

Wine match

The dominance of the rosemary (which gives a piney, woody flavour to this dish) requires a wine that won't be overpowered (too delicate) or turn bitter (oaky).
A favourite last year was the Coume Marie Blanc from Domaine de la Préceptorie in Saint Paul de Fenouillet, AOP Roussillon. La Préceptorie is owned by Marc Parcé, who is one of the three brothers hailing from the famous Domaine de la Rectorie in Banyuls. A fine quality estate and this white wine of theirs is an elegant blend of Grenache Gris, Grenache Blanc, Macabeu and Carignan Blanc. Notes of citrus fruits marry with garrigue and mineral freshness with persistent flavours. This is a wine that continues to evolve in the glass as the evening progresses.

Chorizo aux pois chiches – Chickpeas and chorizo

This is one of those dishes that surprises as the flavours unfold: earthy, spicy, with layers of herbs and piment. You can make it as spicy as you like but note that it is more wine friendly to be restrained! Vegetarians could replace the chorizo with sun blush tomatoes and an extra shake of paprika and piment.

Ingredients

- 200g chickpeas. If you can, use bottled chickpeas as they are superior in quality to the tinned variety, or if you have the time, cook dried peas from scratch
- 250g dried, spicy chorizo
- 1 roasted red pepper
- 1 small red onion finely diced
- 2 cloves of garlic finely chopped
- 1 large handful of fresh oregano, thyme and flat leaf parsley
- Paprika to taste
- Piment d'Espelette
- Seasoning, lemon juice if required
- Plenty of olive oil

Method

1. If using bottled or tinned chickpeas rinse thoroughly.
2. Slice the chorizo into thin rondelles and chop the roasted red pepper. You can buy bottled roasted red peppers easily enough and they are fine, but it is of course better to roast your own as the flavour is much more intense. I make a large batch at a time and keep them in olive oil and garlic in the fridge ready for use.
3. In a large, heavy bottomed frying pan heat a tablespoon of olive oil and gently fry the onion until soft. Add the garlic and chorizo.
4. Once the chorizo starts to colour, add the peppers and chickpeas, turn the heat down as the peas tend to explode and pop all over the place if it is too hot!
5. Gently fry until combined. Add the herbs, paprika, piment and seasoning.
6. Check seasoning, drizzle with oil and, if you feel it needs it, a light squeeze of lemon juice, and serve warm with a green salad or bread.

Wine match

This dish has the combined flavours of the earthy chickpeas, the spicy chorizo and the herbs. It partners well with red wines with good acidity and little, to no, oak. A favourite was Domaine Jean-Baptiste Senat's drolly named Mais Ou Est Il Donc Ornicar! A super elegant wine, that requires food to bring it out of its shell.

Chorizo flambé – Flambéed chorizo and peppers

I got the idea for this from the Food and Travel magazine and then adapted it to suit the flavours of the south. It is very moreish and needs to be served with plenty of crusty bread to sop up the juices.

Ingredients

- 8 fresh chorizo sausages (approx 500g)
- 2 large red peppers
- 5 large garlic cloves
- 1 handful fresh, flat leaf parsley chopped
- 1 small glass of Armagnac

Method

1. Start with chargrilling the peppers. I often do these in batches whenever we are having a barbecue. I just throw them on at the end whilst we are eating, turning from time to time until they are blackened all over. Then pop them into a container with a lid on and allow to cool. Peel and deseed at your leisure, they will last several days in the fridge and over a week if you marinate in olive oil. Alternatively you can char the peppers under a grill or over the gas burner; it's just a bit messy this way!
2. De-skin the chorizo and chop into 2cm round bite-sized slices.
3. Take a heavy bottomed pan (Le Creuset are good) and fry the chorizo until slightly blackened. You will not need to add any extra oil as the sausages will release a lot of natural oil and juices. Pour the juice and oil off from time to time as the chorizo will not blacken if sitting in liquid, you are aiming for a smoky character. You could keep the sausages whole and do them on the barbecue, but I find that they spit and hiss so much that it is easier, if a tad messy, to do it inside on the gas hob!
4. Once the sausages are cooked turn down the heat and add the chopped garlic to the pan to soften, be careful that they don't burn.
5. Peel and deseed the peppers, slice into strips and add to the pan.
6. Cook over a gentle heat for five minutes to combine the flavours.
7. Take a small glass of Armagnac and flambé the chorizo, the Armagnac will set alight, so step back as you do this as so as not to singe your eyebrows! This will give a great flavour without the alcoholic burn.
8. Turn off the heat and stir in the chopped parsley. Serve hot with wooden picks and bread.

Wine match

This is a boldly flavoured dish with spice from the chorizo, so a robust red wine without too much obvious oak works best. Try Les Salines from Domaine des Soulanes, an organic winery in Maury owned by husband and wife team Kathy and Daniel Laffite. It's 85% Grenache and 15% Carignan, elegant with a crisp freshness that works very well with richness of the sausage, but plenty of ripe berry fruit that complements, rather than fights with, the dish.

Soubressade – Spicy sausage tapas

These spicy, orange coloured sausages hail from Spain, and the finest examples come from Mallorca and must state Sobrassada de Mallorca de Cerdo Negro on the label. It is softer, easier to chew than Chorizo, often eaten raw on bread like butter or used in cooking. I created this recipe after tasting something very similar in the pretty seaside town of Collioure, in the Roussillon. There is a lovely, but tiny tapas restaurant, Chez Simone, on the seafront where you can eat delicious dishes whilst gazing out to sea. I tried this when we first moved out to the region, having never heard of Soubressade before, and the waiter kindly gave me the recipe so this is my adaptation of their dish.

Ingredients

- 3 Soubressade sausages
- 2 cloves of garlic
- ½ red pepper
- 1 to 2 tsp smoked paprika

Method

1. Firstly peel the sausages and then roughly chop them into 2cm dice
2. Take a heavy bottomed frying pan and dry fry the sausages. You will find that they release a lot of oil so that there is no need to add any extra. Cook for two minutes.
3. Add the peppers and garlic, and cook for a further two to three minutes until softened; be careful that the garlic doesn't catch and burn.
4. Add the paprika stir well and cook for a further two minutes until everything is thoroughly combined.
5. Remove from the heat and place into a mini food processor and pulse to get a coarse paste consistency.
6. Put into a ceramic serving dish cover and chill
7. Serve on toasts or fresh bread.

Wine match

I usually serve this as part of a platter of charcuterie with saucisson sec, Serrano ham and other patés. As with all of those dishes the Soubressade has a high fat content and so partners well with red wines with crisp acidity to cut through that fat. Something low on tannin and alcohol (not that any wines here in the south are particularly low but it is all relative, not a heady 15%) and without oak. Domaine Gayda's varietal Syrah is a good match. Serve on the cool side, 14°C. Black fruits, pepper and spice with a freshness not dissimilar to the northern Rhone wines.

Brochette et coustellous de porc à la plancha - Pork two ways

Herbed pork ribs

These are delicious eaten hot or cold. You can cook them up on the barbecue and then take them with you on a picnic, and unlike sweet, sticky ribs these are not messy to eat. Make as many as you can manage but they tend to disappear very easily so be generous.

Ingredients

- Short pork ribs, 2 to 4 per person if having as part of a tapas meal, keep the ribs joined together as they are easier to barbecue that way
- 1 tbsp each of chopped thyme, rosemary, oregano and sage
- 1 tbsp Paprika
- 2 large cloves of crushed garlic
- Sea salt and cracked black pepper

Method

1. In a bowl mix together the herbs, paprika, garlic and salt and pepper.
2. Then rub the herb mix into the ribs, massaging it in to every nook and cranny.
3. Put into a container with a lid and leave to marinate for at least two hours but preferably overnight.
4. Light the barbecue and cook the ribs on a medium heat for roughly 20 minutes depending on the ribs' size.
5. Cover and leave to rest for 10 minutes then separate and serve.

Pork brochettes

Allow two pieces per person as part of a tapas meal or double up and serve with saffron rice and grilled courgettes as a main meal. Makes 10 mini brochettes.

Ingredients

- 500g pork escalope cut into 4cm cubes
- 2 cloves of garlic finely chopped
- 1 tbsp Herbs de Provence
- 1/2 tsp Piment d'Espelette
- 2 medium sprigs of fresh rosemary plus 1 for decoration
- 1 tbsp olive oil and extra for drizzling
- 10 wooden brochettes or piques

Method

1. In a bowl mix the marinade ingredients together add the pork and coat thoroughly.
2. Cover and marinate over night.
3. The following day soak the brochettes in water, then thread the pork pieces on.
4. Cook either on a plancha or a barbecue, at a medium heat, brushing with leftover marinade from time to time, for 10 minutes.
5. Serve drizzled with olive oil and a sprig of rosemary.
6. This is nice served with a yoghurt, mint and chive dip and flat breads. If you have a plentiful source of established rosemary you could use rosemary wood as skewers but don't whatever you do decide to get over creative and use Oleander wood as you will poison all your guests!

Wine match

Pork is one of those red meats that can easily match with both red and white wines depending on how you cook it, and the element that links these two pork recipes, (other than the pork obviously), is the herbs. These 'garrigue' style herbs are found growing wild all over the region, they permeate the soil, fill the air with their heady perfume and make their way into the wines. So for these dishes I shall leave you the choice of white and red as they are both a good match. For the white I am heading to the costal appellation of La Clape, just east of Narbonne. The Swiss owned Mas du Soleilla produces a stunning white reserve, a blend of Roussanne and Bourboulenc grapes, made in minuscule quantities. Alternatively if you are looking for a red then further south is the organic Domaine des Schistes in the commune of Tautavel. They produce the Essencial wine, made from a combination of Lledoner Pelut (also known as hairy Grenache!), Syrah and Grenache. Bottled without fining or sulphur, this is as pure as it gets.

Ingredients

- 500g ground meat (equal quantities of beef, sausage and veal is traditional)
- 1 large onion, finely diced
- 3 garlic cloves
- 1 handful of parsley
- 1 large slice of stale bread soaked in milk
- 1 egg
- 800g tomatoes (if using fresh, skinned and seeded)
- 2 medium carrots, finely diced
- 2 tsp paprika
- 1 tsp piment d'esplelette
- Generous pinch of cinnamon
- 200g green olives, stoned
- 50g dried cèpes mushrooms, rehydrated
- Bouquet garni
- 250 ml veal stock
- 60g chopped ham
- Salt and pepper to taste
- Oil for frying

White bean purée

- 800g lingot white beans
- 3 garlic cloves, peeled
- Bouquet garni
- 100ml olive oil
- Chopped parsley
- Lemon juice and seasoning to taste

Method

1. Start by making the sauce. In an oven proof pan heat the oil and gently fry the carrots and half of the onion. Add a pinch of salt to stop the onions browning.
2. Add two of the garlic cloves, the drained mushrooms, bouquet garni, paprika, piment and cinnamon.
3. After a few minutes, when the vegetables have softened, add the tomatoes and the stock. Note that if you are using tinned tomatoes you might want to add a tsp of sugar as they tend to be rather tart.
4. Season and simmer on a low heat whilst you make the meatballs.
5. In a large bowl mix together with your hands the meats, the other half onion finely chopped, minced garlic clove, seasoning and parsley.
6. Squeeze the bread dry and add to the mix with the egg. Mix well.
7. With wet hands (this helps to stop the mix sticking too much) form into meatballs that are roughly the size of a golf ball.
8. Once all the balls are formed you can gently fry them before adding to the sauce, this adds colour and flavour. However I find that if you pop them directly into the sauce and then cook in an oven, at 180°C, you can leave out this time consuming stage without any detriment.
9. Check that the sauce has not thickened too much, if it has add some water, add the olives and ham.
10. Cook for 30 to 40 minutes so that the meat is cooked through and so that the sauce is rich and flavoursome.
11. Serve with a white bean purée.

White bean purée

This makes a good dip as well as an accompaniment.

Method

1. The day before rinse and soak the beans in plenty of cold water.
2. The following day strain and rinse the beans. Put into a large saucepan with the garlic, seasoning, bouquet garni and enough water to cover them.
3. Cook on a medium flame for one and a half hours until cooked.
4. Strain and put into a food processor with the garlic cloves, adding the olive oil to loosen the purée. I find the exact amount of olive oil varies each time so trust your judgement.
5. Check for seasoning, add a squeeze of lemon juice and stir in the parsley.

Wine match

This is a full flavoured dish which is why I am looking to partner it with a wine that is restrained on oak and jammy fruits, as that will be just too much going on. A pub fight in the mouth as it were! Although there are many fabulous wines in the Languedoc to choose from I feel that for this Catalan dish it would be wrong to choose from anywhere other than the Roussillon. The Reliefs from Roc des Anges in Latour de France is undoubtable proof that Carignan can be great, despite the often unfair criticisms. This wine is biodynamic and hails from 100+ year old vines, hand crafted, restrained yet complex with notes of black bramble fruits, spices, wild mushroom and a long mineral finish.

Boles de Picolat – Catalan meatballs

This is a Catalan dish and when you cross the border from the Languedoc to the Roussillon you see these being sold in all the restaurants and markets. You can make the balls smaller and serve as a tapas dish with piques and bread or with the traditional accompaniment, a purée of garlicky white beans.

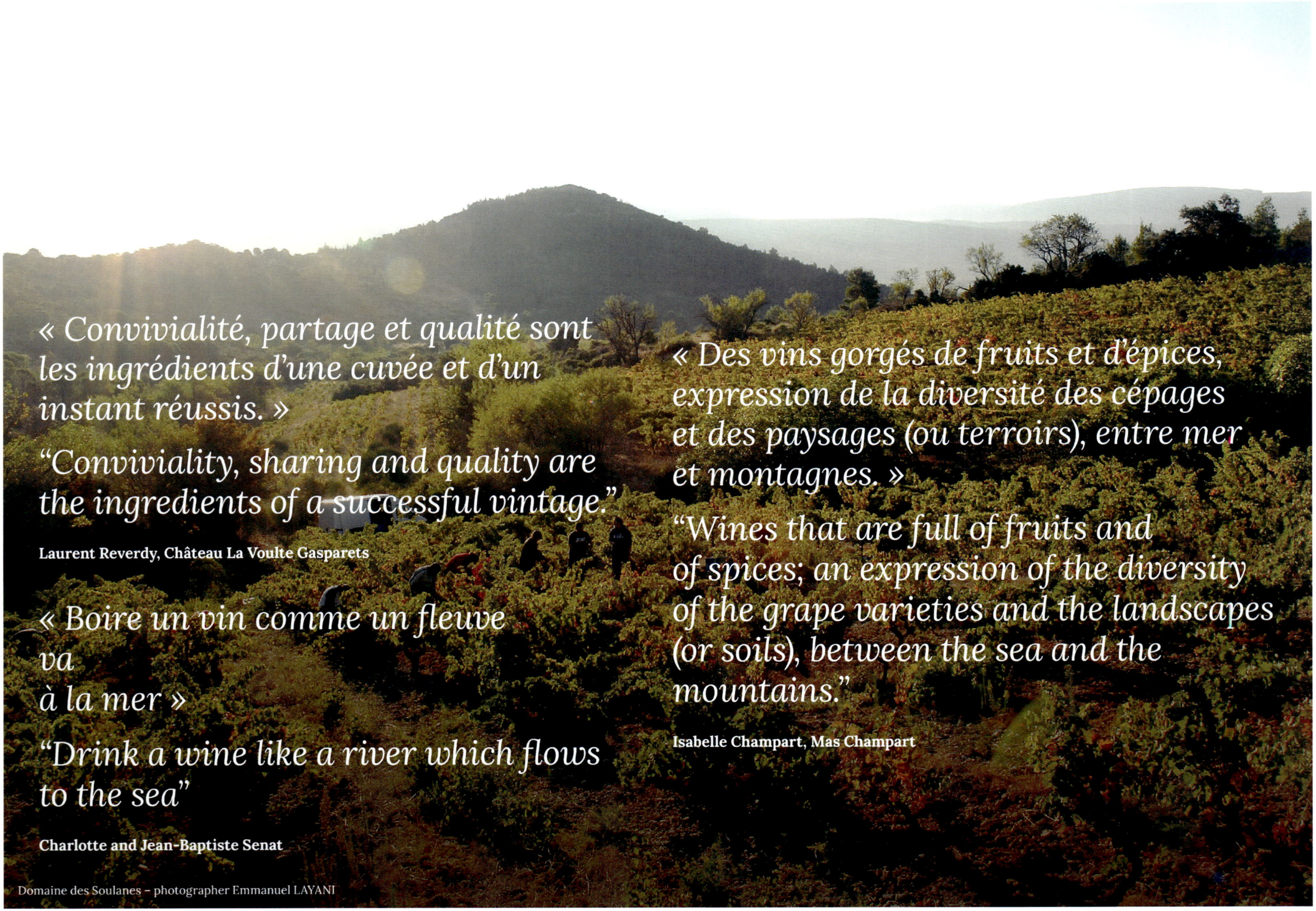

« Convivialité, partage et qualité sont les ingrédients d'une cuvée et d'un instant réussis. »

"Conviviality, sharing and quality are the ingredients of a successful vintage."

Laurent Reverdy, Château La Voulte Gasparets

« Boire un vin comme un fleuve
va
à la mer »

"Drink a wine like a river which flows to the sea"

Charlotte and Jean-Baptiste Senat

« Des vins gorgés de fruits et d'épices, expression de la diversité des cépages et des paysages (ou terroirs), entre mer et montagnes. »

"Wines that are full of fruits and of spices; an expression of the diversity of the grape varieties and the landscapes (or soils), between the sea and the mountains."

Isabelle Champart, Mas Champart

Domaine des Soulanes – photographer Emmanuel LAYANI

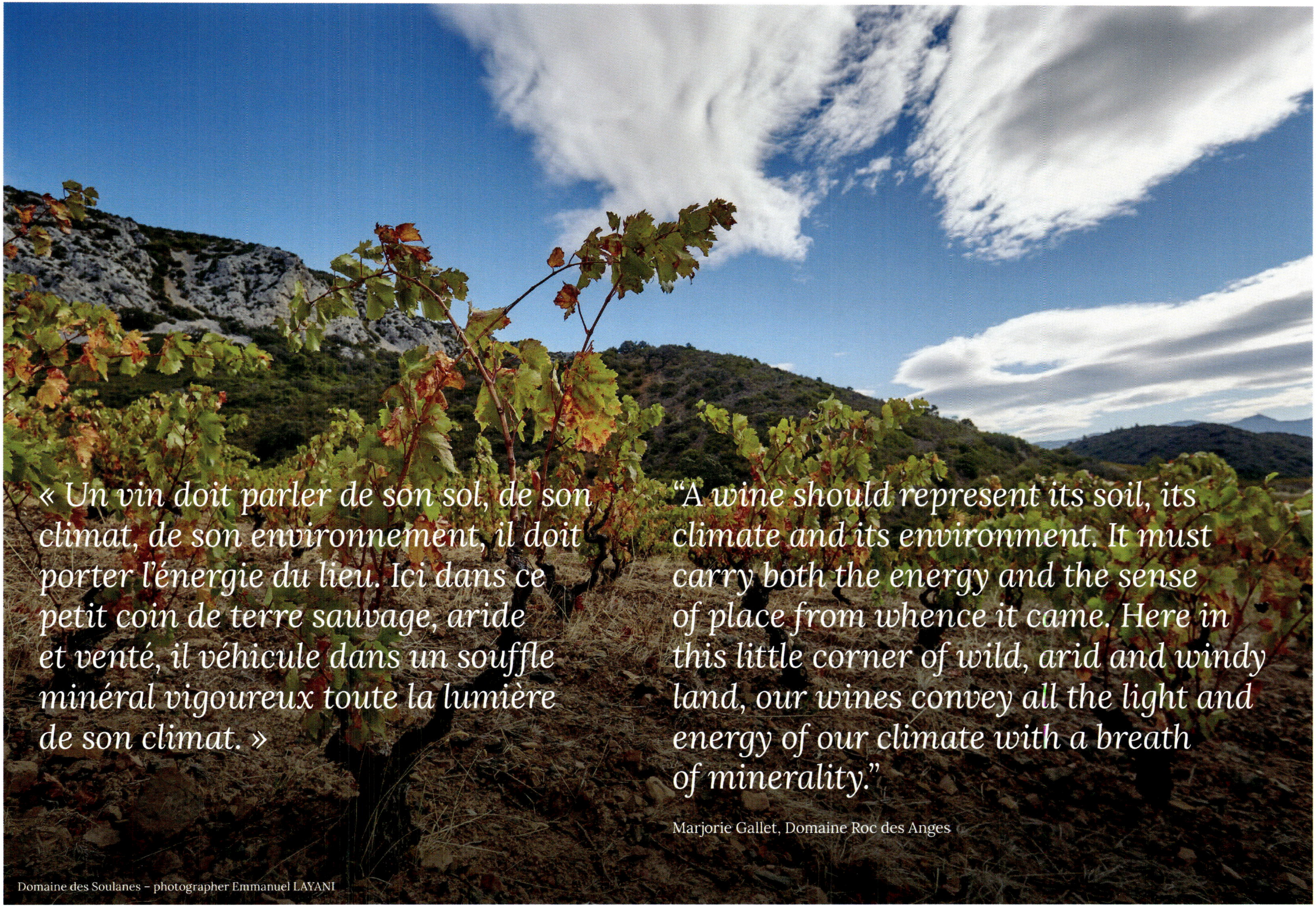

« Un vin doit parler de son sol, de son climat, de son environnement, il doit porter l'énergie du lieu. Ici dans ce petit coin de terre sauvage, aride et venté, il véhicule dans un souffle minéral vigoureux toute la lumière de son climat. »

"A wine should represent its soil, its climate and its environment. It must carry both the energy and the sense of place from whence it came. Here in this little corner of wild, arid and windy land, our wines convey all the light and energy of our climate with a breath of minerality."

Marjorie Gallet, Domaine Roc des Anges

Domaine des Soulanes – photographer Emmanuel LAYANI

The duck here needs to be of the finest quality as really there is very little cooking involved. It is more about showing off the quality of the bird and the symmetry with the wine. One duck breast yields approximately 20 slices, which should be cut very thinly. You could serve a slice on a slice of potato poached in duck fat, with a dollop of the sauce as a tapas. If having as a main meal count two generous portions per breast.

Magret de canard sauce Carignan - Duck breast with a Carignan sauce

Ingredients

- 1 duck magret (for a reliable source look for the AOP Sud-Ouest de France label)
- 1 large garlic clove
- Rock salt and black pepper
- Rosemary

Sauce

- 1 heaped tbsp of Carignan jelly (see below)
- 500ml duck (chicken) stock
- 100ml Carignan based red wine
- 1 small onion
- 1 clove garlic
- 2 sprigs of rosemary
- Cornflour to thicken
- Seasoning

Method

1. To prepare the duck firstly cut off any sinewy bits and overlapping skin.
2. With a sharp knife make criss-cross incisions on the skin, being careful not to cut right through the skin.
3. Then rub the skin and flesh with the garlic, plenty of salt, pepper and chopped rosemary.
4. Take a heavy bottomed pan and set over a medium heat. Turn on the extractor, open the windows and have a ceramic dish at hand to strain off any excess fat.
5. Then once the pan is hot, place the duck skin side down into the pan, pressing down with the tongs so that all of the skin is touching the pan.
6. Make sure that you drain off the duck fat often as otherwise it will spit like mad and make a terrible mess!
7. Once the skin is browned turn over and cook the underside, always pressing down so that the breast is touching the pan all over.
8. With the tongs pick up the breast and brown on both edges.
9. Turn back over to the skin side down and finish off.
10. Remove from the pan and leave to rest for at least 10 minutes. If you like your meat well done you can cover the duck and this will continue to cook it. However magret is best served rare to preserve the delicate flavour and texture.
11. Slice and serve with the sauce drizzled over it.
12. You can enjoy this duck with either Sardalaise potatoes (sliced potatoes cooked in duck fat and garlic) or herby Puy lentils.

The sauce

1. Put the stock, wine, vegetables and rosemary into a pan and bring to the boil.
2. Reduce the heat and simmer until reduced by a third.
3. Add the grape jelly and seasoning. Taste and adjust the amount of jelly and seasoning accordingly.
4. If the sauce is too runny, thicken with cornflour ensuring that you cook it for at least 10 minutes to get rid of any flour taste.
5. This duck and sauce can be served hot or cold, as you prefer. If serving cold the sauce is better thicker rather than too thin.

The jelly

1. If you are lucky enough to be given tons of juicy grapes during harvest time as I am, you can make your own grape jelly. You simply de-stalk the grapes, put them into a saucepan over a low heat and mash from time to time with a potato masher. This will release the juice. It takes about 20 minutes of gentle heating and occasional mashing.
2. Remove from the heat and strain the juice (you can leave this overnight) into a jug through a sieve lined with a jelly bag, mashing all the pulp as you go.
3. Measure the juice, you should get roughly 600ml for a kilo of grapes. Pour the juice into a jam pam with 450g preserving sugar with added pectin.
4. Bring to the boil and cook until it reaches 105C. If you don't have a thermometer put a saucer in the freezer and pour some of the jam onto the saucer; if the jam wrinkles when you run your finger through it, it is ready. If not, heat some more.
5. Pour into sterilised jars with a sprig of rosemary.

Note: You can replace the grape jelly with redcurrant jelly.

Wine match

The strong flavour of the duck, combined with the richness of the fat, is already balanced by the slight sweetness of the sauce. The wine here needs to be full flavoured and intense but not too oaky or alcoholic. There are many wines that I have used in the past with this dish and they were all delicious in their own right. Try the Lema from Domaine de Roquemale in the Grès de Montpellier. It is a heady mix of Syrah, Grenache and Mourvèdre with red fruit and liquorice flavours with a herbal finish. Roquemale is the Occitan for 'bad stone', so called due to the harsh limestone and clay stones that the vines grow on.

Gigot d'agneau à la cuillère – Slow roast lamb with lentils

Ingredients

- 1 leg of lamb
- 2 onions, sliced
- 2 carrots, roughly diced
- 2 medium sized leeks or fennel, depending on what's available, roughly diced
- 8 garlic cloves, sliced
- 4 anchovy fillets
- 1 bottle of white wine, for example a VDP Chardonnay
- 1 tin of chopped tomatoes
- 2 bay leaves
- Rosemary sprigs
- 1 tbsp of rosemary and thyme, picked and chopped
- 200g green lentils, Puy or Lauragais, rinsed
- 200g Agen prunes, de-stoned and chopped in half
- Pepper

When I make this for my tastings I am usually cooking tapas sized portions for eight to 12 people. I tend to use a smaller cut of lamb, such as a piece of shoulder, and reduce the cooking time. However if I was doing this at home I would use a gigot (leg) of lamb and serve for a long, lazy Sunday lunch shared with friends.

Serves 8 as a main course

Method

1. Heat the oven to 120°C
2. Take your leg of lamb and remove any sinews. Make a dozen slits on each side and poke a slice of garlic and either a sliver of anchovy or a sprig of rosemary in each hole.
3. Take a heavy pan with a lid and layer the onion on the base. Place the gigot onto the onion bed and cover with the wine and tomatoes. Add black pepper (no salt as the anchovies will add saltiness), herbs and bay leaves. Put the lid on and put in the oven.
4. Every hour or so turn the lamb and add a glass of water to the pot if the sauce is starting to dry out.
5. After 3 to 4 hours (depending on the size of your gigot) add the vegetables, lentils and prunes to the pan. You may need to add more liquid at this point. Turn the heat up to 150°C.
6. After 40 minutes check the lentils, they should be cooked but still firm. You may need to cook for longer.
7. Remove from the oven and take the lamb out of the dish. It will probably be falling off the bone but don't worry if it falls apart as this dish is served 'à la cuillière' (with a spoon).
8. Strain the vegetables and lentils, arrange on a plate with the lamb on top. There is no need to rest the lamb.
9. Skim off any fat from the top of the sauce and check for seasoning. Reduce if it is too liquid.
10. Serve the sauce with the lamb and lentils. The lamb should be meltingly soft and the lentils and vegetables al dente.

Wine match

Lamb is a very wine friendly meat and this combination of slow cooking with herbs and wine is a taste sensation. With this style of cooking I tend to err on the side of caution and choose a red wine that is not too bold in flavours, something more subtle but complex. I should probably move to Calce as I am heading back there to suggest a wine from Gèrard Gauby this time, Muntada. Another outstanding wine, made using biodynamic techniques and displaying great restraint. The resulting wine is elegant and sublime. It is made from old Grenache, Syrah, Mourvèdre and Carignan vines ranging from 15 to 120 years old. This is a special occasion wine and hence should be served with a special dish. A match made in heaven!

Gâteau aux amandes - Almond cake

Everyone should have a fall-back cake and this is mine. Super quick and easy to make, and you can adapt by adding or changing spices, lemon zest and even chocolate. There are only four key ingredients, so get the best quality you can.

Ingredients

- 200g whole almonds in their skins
- 4 eggs, if very large reduce to 3
- 100g melted butter. Although most chefs would disagree with me I always use salted as I like the richness
- 200g fine sugar
- Pinch of vanilla powder or ground ginger to taste

Method

1. Heat the oven to 200°C, butter and line a 20cm square cake tin.
2. Melt the butter over a gentle heat, then cool.
3. Grind the almonds in a food processor. You can use already ground almonds but I much prefer the texture and flavour of whole almonds in their skins ground coarsely.
4. In a bowl mix together the almonds, butter and sugar with a wooden spoon.
5. Add the eggs one by one. Sometimes the eggs I get from the market are very large and so I only use three. Mix in well.
6. Add the vanilla or ginger to taste.
7. Pour into the prepared cake tin and bake for approximately 20 minutes until a skewer comes out clean.
8. Leave to cool in the tin then transfer onto a rack.
9. Serve on its own, with strawberries or with a dollop of crème fraîche.
10. Variations can include different spices, you could add the zest and juice of a lemon (it will be much moister so reduce the eggs to three) or you could melt 100g of dark chocolate with the butter.

Wine match

This is a lightly flavoured cake, with the pleasing texture of the home-ground almonds. The Languedoc-Roussillon is famous for its Vins Doux Naturel sweet wines. Heady wines that are fortified and made in a similar style to Port, usually made from Muscat or Grenache. However Sarrat de Goundy, in La Clape, make a rare, unfortified, 100% Muscat wine. Deliciously light and fabulous fruity, full of honeysuckle and peach flavours. Coming in at only 12% ABV it is a perfect afternoon wine!

Soupe de fraises – Strawberry soup

The strawberry season starts in March here, and I was amazed at all the different varieties of strawberries that are available at the market, having grown up knowing only a choice of English, Kent or Spanish. I have since found out that there are over 600 different varieties of strawberry. Choose a full flavoured variety and very ripe for this soup. I use Gariguette early in the season and Charlotte in the height of summer. It works very well with a slice of almond and lemon cake, just add the zest and juice of a lemon to the recipe already given.

Ingredients

- 250g strawberries, washed and hulled
- 2 tbsp icing sugar
- 1 large sprig of mint, the leaves only
- 1 small glass of Muscat
- Water and ice

Method

1. Put the first four ingredients into a blender and blitz until smooth.
2. Add a few cubes of ice and water to loosen, blend again.
3. Taste, depending on the ripeness and variety of strawberries chosen you may need to add more sugar.
4. The resulting soup should be sweet, but not cloying, with just a hint of mint and Muscat.
5. Chill and serve in tea cups or shot glasses.
6. This recipe is very easy to double, or even treble. I have given quantities enough for eight shot glasses but at home you might want to have a larger portion!

Wine match

This is a perfect match for a Muscat wine. The Domaine Jones is a favourite because of the low alcohol. However a Muscat from St Jean de Minervois is equally delightful. Clos de Gravaillas is an organic Domaine owned by a local girl, Nicole, and husband John, from Kentucky. Their dessert wine Douce Providence is a 100% Muscat de Petits Grains with 125g/l of residual sugar and 15% ABV. A delightful wine with notes of pineapple and rose petals. Serve chilled.

Pain d'épice – Spiced cake

Ingredients

- 250g flour
- 60g soft brown sugar
- 150g honey. You can really change the flavour depending on what type of honey you use; in colder months I quite like to use a chestnut honey that gives a dark, slightly bitter edge. Alternatively, sunflower honey is the least pungent and works better in the summer.
- 100ml milk
- 2tsp fleur d'oranger
- 1 tsp bicarbonate of soda
- 2 tsp pain d'épice spice mix (I usually make my own; a blend of ginger, cinnamon, cloves and aniseed. Go gently with the last two though as they can easily dominate)
- 70g butter
- 2 eggs
- 200g dates
- 1 small glass of Armagnac

This pungent spiced bread originates from Alsace and was traditionally made using just rye flour, honey and spices. Over the years it has become more commercial and more cake-like. This is my version that I adapted from Chef Simone at Le Monde. I also like to add dates soaked in Armagnac; very untraditional, but very nice.

Method

1. The day before, de-pip and roughly chop the dates, put them into a plastic container with a lid and cover in the Armagnac. Shake and leave to soak overnight.
2. Preheat the oven to 170°C, butter and line a tin. It is normal to use a loaf tin however I often use a 20 x 20cm cake tin and cut the cake into small squares.
3. In a saucepan over a gentle heat melt the butter, honey, sugar and milk; be careful not to boil it.
4. In a large mixing bowl sieve the flour, bicarbonate and spices.
5. Add the melted butter mix to the flour, along with the fleur d'oranger and dates and Armagnac. Stir thoroughly with a wooden spoon to combine.
6. Add the eggs and beat thoroughly, check that everything is completely mixed in and transfer to your prepared tin.
7. Cook in the oven, if you are using a loaf tin it will take approximately 40 minutes, however a cake tin takes less, normally 30 minutes.
8. Remove from the oven when a skewer comes out clean and cool on a wire rack.
9. If wrapped in greaseproof paper and kept in a tin this will stay moist for the best part of a week. If it gets a bit dry you could serve it with some butter, just don't tell the French!

Wine match

The Vins Doux Naturels found in this region are just a perfect match for this heavily spiced cake, in particular the ambré wines from Rivesaltes. These are wines that have been aged on ullage for several years, resulting in an evaporation of 7% of the volume which intensifies the nutty, dried fruit character in the wine and turns it 'amber' in colour. Notes of caramel, pain d'épice, dates and walnuts abound. Domaine Cazes do some fantastic examples, but the Caves at Agly do a surprisingly enjoyable version, Château Montner 2002 hit just the right notes of rich sweetness and spicy nuttiness.

Petits pots au chocolat – Chocolate pots

Ingredients

- 250ml creme fluide (single cream can work but just reduce the sugar. I often use soya cream it has a nice texture and you don't taste the 'soya' flavour).
- 100g 70% dark chocolate, the best quality you can get
- Sugar to taste, roughly count 1 heaped teaspoon per person but I suggest you taste and adjust to your preferred level of sweetness. We like it quite dark.
- A pinch of vanilla powder
- A pinch or ground ginger

It is impossible for me to remember how this recipe came about; I had been trying out various versions of chocolate pots from various chefs, French and English, and they were all too fiddly or time consuming. I needed a super easy, delicious chocolate dessert for those chocolate emergencies and here it is. My boy Louis' favourite dessert!

Serves four gourmands or six small portions. Eight is a bit too mean in this case.

Method

1. Gently heat the cream and sugar in a heavy bottomed pan until the sugar dissolves. Do not boil.
2. Remove from the heat and add the chocolate, let it sit for a minute or two and then beat briskly with a wooden spoon until smooth.
3. Add the spices and check the sweetness level, if you find that it is not sweet enough for your taste I recommend adding a squeeze of agave sirop now as it won't change the flavour and doesn't need to melt.
4. Pour into espresso cups and place into the fridge to set. Two hours should do it, but the longer you leave it the more set they will be. If you find you are doing it at the last minute just serve with some biscuits, langue de chat, biscotti, and no one will know that they were supposed to be anything other than liquid.
5. You can add different flavourings if you like. In winter I like to add some orange zest and if Louis isn't having any, a touch of Cointreau (I suppose orange juice would work.) But on the whole I think that the success of this dish is in its simplicity.

Wine match

One of the best matches with this was when I cracked open an old bottle of Pedro Ximenez with some friends. But although close it isn't from the Languedoc-Roussillon so another super match was with Domaine Cazes' Grenat Vin Doux Naturel (VDN) – a regional speciality, fortified red wine made from the Grenache grape. This wine is unctuous without being cloying. Domaine Cazes are the largest biodynamic winery in Europe with over 300ha, and whilst they have an extensive range of wines it is their VDN wines that really stand out in my opinion.

Petits carrés au chocolat – Chocolate fruit and nut squares

This is really an adult version of a fridge cake and came about by accident when I was experimenting with flavours and textures one day. It was so popular that I would serve it at tastings and dinner parties, it also makes a good gift at Christmas.

Ingredients

- 200g good quality 70% dark chocolate
- 1 tbsp golden syrup, you could use agave syrup
- 1 tbsp salted butter
- 1 handful of chopped prunes soaked in Armagnac overnight
- 1 handful of almonds, roughly chopped
- 3 to 4 cubes of crystallised ginger, chopped (the strength can vary enormously here so put in as little or as much as you personally like)
- 1 tsp ground ginger

Method

1. Place a heat proof glass bowl over a pan of simmering water and melt the chocolate with the butter and syrup. Take care that the water doesn't boil and that the bowl does not touch the water.
2. Once melted add all the other ingredients and mix well.
3. Line a square cake tin with greaseproof paper and pour the chocolate mix into it, pushing down with a spatula to get an even layer.
4. Chill in the fridge overnight.
5. The following day remove from the tin and cut into bite sized pieces. Depending on the size of tin you used you should get around 24 pieces.
6. Store in an airtight tin in the fridge.

Wine match

Chocolate and Vins Doux Naturels is a fabulous combination. Serve these with a lightly chilled glass of Domaine Bertha Maillol's Banyuls. They do several but I would recommend the youthful version for this match, the Rimage. A 100% Grenache at 17% ABV, a delicious combination of blackberries, cherries and prunes.

Pruneaux enrobés de chocolat – Chocolate prunes

This is the perfect finish to a wine and tapas tasting; just that edge of sweetness without being cloying, and regardless of how full you are there is always room for just one little chocolate covered prune... or maybe two!

Ingredients

- 500g Agen Prunes, whole and de-stoned
- 250ml Armagnac
- 250g good quality dark chocolate. I use an organic 70% from the Dominican Republic. Quality chocolate should never be black and even at 70% will not be bitter. It is worth spending a bit more.
- Greaseproof paper

Method

1. If you bought prunes with their stone in remove them whilst trying to retain their shape.
2. Prick the skins with a fork, put into a large Kilner jar (or Tupperware) and cover with the Armagnac and leave for as long as possible, but at least overnight.
3. Put the jar in a dark corner of the kitchen, cool but not forgotten and shake from time to time as you go past.
4. When ready, melt the chocolate in a bowl over a pan of steaming water, taking care that the bowl doesn't touch the water as the chocolate could seize – that is turn lumpy and grainy. Chocolate can seize if it gets too hot in the bowl, or if any water is splashed into it by mistake.
5. When melted remove from the heat but keep the hot water close by in case you need to melt the chocolate again.
6. Roll out the greaseproof paper onto a baking tray, then with clean hands gently dip the prunes into the melted chocolate. Be careful not to burn your fingers and resist the temptation to lick them!
7. Place the chocolate covered prunes onto the greaseproof paper and place in a cool, dark place to set. You could put them in the fridge, but note that cheap chocolate will turn white!
8. Once set, put into an airtight container.
9. These prunes have the ability to age for a long time, but they rarely get the chance!

Wine match

Chocolate is a hard one to match due to its coating qualities. This is where the fine wines of Banyuls excel. Domaine de la Rectorie produce some outstanding examples, such as their Cuvée Leon Parcé which has just the perfect combination of fruit, balanced sweetness and intense flavours.

List of wine producers

Domaine Antech	Limoux, 11300	http://www.antech-limoux.com
Domaine Berta Maillol	Banyuls sur Mer, 66650	http://www.bertamaillol.com
Domaine Cazes	Rivesaltes, 66600	https://www.cazes-rivesaltes.com/
Mas Champart	St Chinian, 34360	https://www.mas-champart.com/
Domaine Clos du Gravaillas	Saint Jean de Minervois, 34360	https://www.closdugravillas.com
Colline de L'Hirondelle	Douzens, 11700	http://collinedelhirondelle.com
Domaine des Deux Clés	Fontjoncouse, 11360	http://en.domaine-des-deux-cles.com
Domaine Gauby	Calce, 66600	http://www.domainegauby.fr
Domaine Gayda	Brugaroilles, 11300	http://www.gaydavineyards.com
Domaine de L'Hortus	Val du Montferrand, 34270	http://www.domaine-hortus.fr
Domaine Jones	Tuchan, 11350	http://www.domainejones.com
Laurent Miquel	Cessenon sur Orb, 34460	http://www.laurent-miquel.com
Domaine Matassa	Montner, 66720	https://www.matassawine.fr
Château Montner	Estagel, 66310	http://agly.fr
Domaine Mouscaillo	Roquetaillade, 11300	http://www.mouscaillo.com
Domaine Ollier Taillefer	Fos, 34320	http://olliertaillefer.com
Domaine Olivier Pithon	Calce, 66600	http://www.olivierpithon.com
Domaine Pierre Clavel	Assas, 34820	https://www.facebook.com/pierre.clavel.921
Domaine de la Preceptorie	Saint Paul de Fenouillet, 66220	http://www.la-preceptorie.com
Domaine de la Rectorie	Banyuls sur Mer, 66650	http://www.rectorie.com
Château Rives Blanques	Cépie, 11300	http://www.rives-blanques.com
Domaine Roc des Anges	Latour de France, 66720	http://marjorie-stephane-gallet.com
Domaine Roquemale	Villeveyrac, 34560	https://www.roquemale.com
Domaine de la Rune	Talairan, 11220	http://www.domainelarune.com
Domaine Sarrat de Goundy	La Clape, 11110	http://www.sarratdegoundy.fr
Domaine des Schistes	Estagel, 66310	https://domainedesschistes.com
Domaine Senat	Trausse, 11160	http://www.domaine-senat.com
Mas du Soleilla	La Clape, 11110	http://www.mas-du-soleilla.fr
Domaine des Soulanes	Tautavel, 66720	http://www.domaine-soulanes.com
Château La Voulte Gasparets	Boutenac, 11200	http:/www.lavoultegasparets.com

Photographs courtsey of the Domaines, see page 44

Photography

Garth Bowden

Garth Bowden is a British artist and designer based in Paris and the south of France. Garth has a multi-disciplinary practice combining painting, sculpture, design and photography.

He has recently exhibited in the UK, France, Germany, French Polynesia and Switzerland.

Garth has a BA in Fine Art from Chelsea School of Art, London.

www.garthbowden.com

www.garthbowdendesign.com

I have known Garth since I moved to the Languedoc-Roussillon. He was the first person that Chris and I met, as it was he that let us in to our rented accommodation back in 2008. He is an extremely talented artist, with a keen eye for design. It was both great fun and a privilege to work with him on this project; his photographs are truly stunning.

Thanks Gaffa!

Credits

Many thanks to the following wine domaines for giving their kind permission to use their photographs in this book, as shown on front cover, 5, 30, 62, 63 and 79.

Mas Champart

Colline de l'Hirondelle

Domaine des Deux Clés – photographer Medienagenten & Andreas Durst

Domaine Jones

Domaine Mouscaillo

Domaine Ollier Taillefer

Domaine de la Rectorie

Château Rives-Blanques

Domaine de Roc des Anges

Domaine Senat

Domaine des Soulanes – photographer Emmanuel LAYANI

Château La Voulte Gasparets